With Net and Coble

With Net and Coble

A Salmon Fisher on the Cromarty Firth

George Chamier

PEN & SWORD
HISTORY

First published in Great Britain in 2021 by
Pen & Sword History
An imprint of
Pen & Sword Books Ltd
Yorkshire – Philadelphia

ISBN 978 1 39901 495 3

A CIP catalogue record for this book is
available from the British Library.

Typeset by Mac Style
Printed and bound in the UK by CPI Group (UK) Ltd, Croydon, CR0 4YY.

Pen & Sword Books Limited incorporates the imprints of Atlas, Archaeology,
Aviation, Discovery, Family History, Fiction, History, Maritime, Military,
Military Classics, Politics, Select, Transport, True Crime, Air World, Frontline
Publishing, Leo Cooper, Remember When, Seaforth Publishing, The Praetorian
Press, Wharncliffe Local History, Wharncliffe Transport, Wharncliffe True
Crime and White Owl.

For a complete list of Pen & Sword titles please contact

PEN & SWORD BOOKS LIMITED
47 Church Street, Barnsley, South Yorkshire, S70 2AS, England
E-mail: enquiries@pen-and-sword.co.uk
Website: www.pen-and-sword.co.uk

Or

PEN AND SWORD BOOKS
1950 Lawrence Rd, Havertown, PA 19083, USA
E-mail: Uspen-and-sword@casematepublishers.com
Website: www.penandswordbooks.com

To all fishers of salmon, both anglers and netsmen

Contents

Introduction		ix
Maps		xiii
1	A Balconie Day	1
2	Catching the Fish	7
3	An Alness Day	18
4	Himself	22
5	Going Solo	37
6	A Flash of Wings …	43
7	At Balconie	46
8	Netting the Scottish Fish	64
9	Fisher Men	65
10	A Million Hands Clapping	68
11	Early Days	70
12	The Firth	80
13	Diaries	86
14	A Couple of Good Weeks	89
15	A July Morning	92
16	At the Fishing	96
17	At Alness	99
18	An Evening High Water	103
19	East Wind on the Beach	105
20	Ardroy	107

21   Nigg   110

22   Tide, Wind and Water   114

23   The River with Three Names   123

24   Fish in Trouble   127

25   The Salmon in the Glass Case   135

26   Rods versus Nets   136

27   A Photographer at the Fishing   140

28   At Kiltearn   145

29   The Last Good Tide   160

30   The Biologists   161

31   The Other Fishers   164

32   Poached Salmon   171

33   A Kiltearn Morning   174

34   Decline and Fall   179

35   Reflections   183

36   The Last Fishers   187

Glossary   188
Acknowledgements   191

Introduction

Thousands of books have been written about salmon fishing, and hundreds more books and articles appear every year. Reminiscences of great fishing days; where to fish and where to catch the biggest fish (it used to be Norway, now it's Russia); how to tie flies, which flies to use, how to induce fish to take them and how to 'play' your fish once you have hooked him.

This is not one of those books. There'll be no exciting battles with thirty-pounders, none of the pawky wit of Highland ghillies, the camaraderie of the river bank, the roaring fires and exhaustive malt whisky collections of the finest fishing hotels. This is a book about catching salmon not with rod and line, but with net and coble. Many salmon anglers blench at the mention of netting their treasured fish: it's unfair, unsporting, too easy and, worst of all, blamed for declining numbers. Over the years, I have enjoyed appalling not a few tweedy chaps by opening a discussion of salmon fishing and then revealing, at a crucial moment, that I am a netsman.

There is, of course, netting and netting, everything from the quietly and illegally set private net in a river pool or estuary to the big commercial operations of yesteryear – the Paterson family of Easter Ross, say, whose bag net stations employed seventy men; the Northumberland drift-netters, who intercepted so many fish heading for Scottish rivers; or the really big oceanic operators who took a huge tonnage of fish off the Faroes and Greenland. But our sort of fishing is none of these. What we do, or used to anyway, is sweep-netting, otherwise known as 'net and coble', or 'beach seine' if you are going to be technical about it. Not that sweep-netting can't be deadly, too, if practised at the mouth of big rivers where fish congregate in great numbers when the run is on. The sweep nets at Bonar Bridge, where the Oykel, Shin, Cassley and Carron, fine salmon rivers all, flow in a single channel through the Kyle of Sutherland into the Dornoch Firth, were taking some 10,000 fish annually even in the 1980s.

We never took as many as that. On the stations in the Cromarty Firth where I worked in the 1960s, 70s and 80s, we looked for a thousand, or two in a good year. And there is something very different about the way we fish. On a standard sweep-netting station it is simply a question of rowing the net round time after time, trusting to luck that it will intercept fish. We tend to regard this method with scorn. On some stations, especially those which used to operate within a river, there were ways of telling when fish are coming: a shallows, perhaps, where fish show, a rope in the water to make them jump, a high seat for a watcher to look down into the water. There was even a station we once visited on the west coast where the fishermen reckoned their collie could see fish coming. But our sort of fishing is none of these. The way we fish, the skill that excites us and keeps us coming back to it year after year, is that we don't just spot the fish, we follow them by eye: we have learned to track them by the mark they make on the surface as they swim high in the water and so can row our shot precisely to intercept them.

We are able to do this because we fish near the mouth of a river where there is fresh water mixing with the salt of the firth. Fresh water is what the fish are looking for; they are returning from the open sea to spawn in the rivers. And fresh water, being less dense than salt, collects in streaks at the surface. If it was all salt or all fresh, then he would swim too deep to crease the surface. If we were fishing in open water, then the swell would mask the signs. But of course you have to learn what you are looking for. When the water is calm and the light is right, anyone can see fish – that is, if you can tell which mark is fish and which is a shoal of sprats, a puff of wind or the water left behind by a sea trout jumping. What we like best is a light but steady breeze which creates a uniform ripple; then the eye is quickly taken by anything breaking the pattern, although a practised hand can see fish in almost any water except a gale. It is easier looking downwind, because then he will put up more of a water swimming towards you against the waves, but you can see a big head of fish – twenty or thirty, say – almost anywhere. Still they are not often plain to see, and to an outsider the operation can look like magic.

*   *   *

As in many passages in the rest of the book, I find myself writing in the present tense, as if we were still fishing. And it is extraordinary to me that we are not. From 1975 to 2018, and for five years in the 1960s, there wasn't a single summer that did not find me on the firth, watching for fish. But there are almost no salmon netsmen in Scotland now. Fishing rights have been bought out, by angling or conservation bodies, and the fishing stations closed down; coastal fixed nets have been banned by law since 2015; the drift nets and high seas fisheries have gone, too; and most sweep-netting stations have been put out of business as a result of conservation regulations. All that remain in Scotland are a few Solway Firth haaf-netters, a traditional method used down there, and a handful of 'hobby' sweep-netters. An era has ended.

To make sense of this book, which dots about between times and places, it may be helpful to the reader to give an outline of my fishing life:

1964–68	Learning the fishing from Buller Black at Balconie for a few weeks each summer in school holidays or university vacations as the 'loon' at the height of the season.
1969-75	Working in advertising in London and Amsterdam. No fishing.
1975–79	Skippering the fishing at Balconie with the 'Balconie Babes' (Eddie and Stevie Web). Buller fishing a half share at Alness until 1987.

1980–83	Set up Ardroy Fisheries to rent the other half share at Alness.
	Fished Alness (with Doug) and Balconie on alternate days.
1984–85	Fished Nigg in July with a big crew, otherwise at Balconie.
1986–87	Fished Balconie with various crew.
1987	Rights to Balconie bought out by the District Fishery Board and station closed down. Alness station also closed.
	Moved south and started working as a teacher. My full-time fishing life (1975–87) comes to an end. From now on I am a part-time hobby fisherman, for six weeks or so each summer.
1988–99	Fished Foulis/Kiltearn with Doug as skipper.
2000–18	Skippered Kiltearn. Main crew first Rik, then Rod and Jonathan.
2005–	Retired from teaching and moved to London. Still fishing every summer.
2018	Marine Scotland declares the firth a mandatory catch and release zone. The fishing comes to an end.

Watching the water for fish. (*RR*)

If you don't know the area, consult the first map. And then, unless you know the fishing, have a look at the second. Technical fishing terms and Scots words which may be unfamiliar to some readers are included in the glossary.

One more thing. As the Scottish Wildlife Trust put it in a recent article, 'Numbers [of salmon] are at critically low levels, and urgent and meaningful conservation action is needed.' This book contains a lot of descriptions of catching and killing salmon, in numbers that may sometimes seem gross to a modern reader. I make no apology for this. For a good bit of my fishing life there was a legitimately harvestable surplus of fish, and we were doing it for a living. In more recent years it became a hobby, and we caught very few. And as I hope the book makes clear, it wasn't just about the catching of fish.

Indeed, we carried on doing it when we were hardly catching any at all. It was an addiction, a way of life, and the happiness of being in a beautiful place.

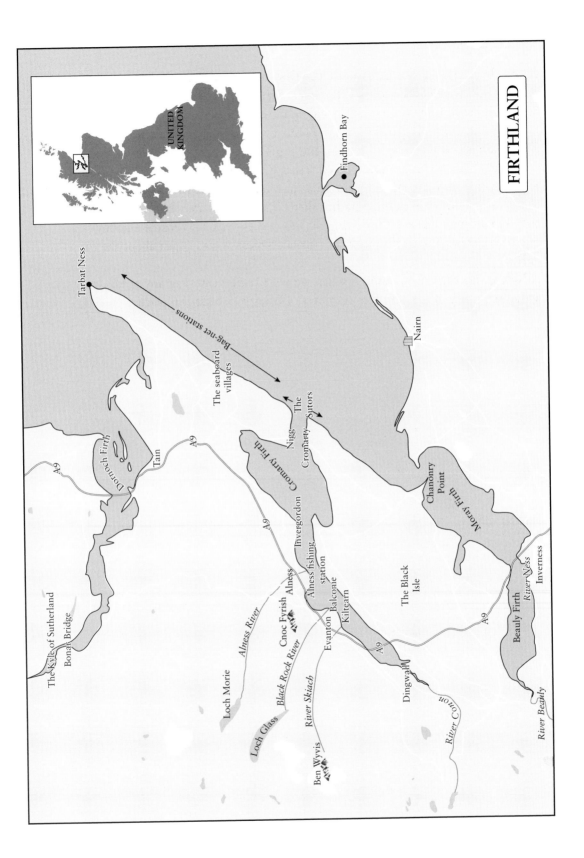

FIRTHLAND

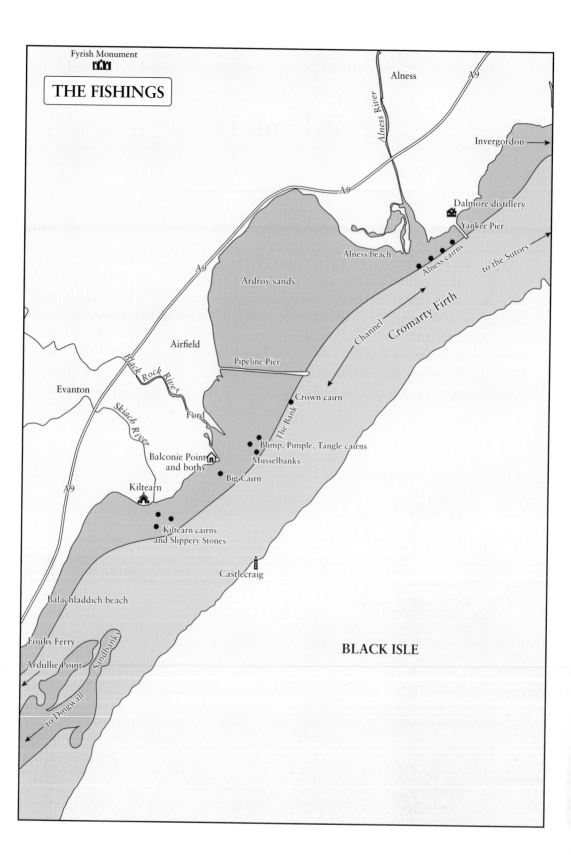

Fyrish Monument

THE FISHINGS

Alness

Alness River

A9

Invergordon

A9

Dalmore distillery

Yankee Pier

Alness beach

Alness cairns

to the Sutors

Ardroy sands

Channel

Cromarty Firth

Airfield

Black Rock River

Pipeline Pier

Evanton

Skiach River

Ford

Crown cairn

The Bank

Balconie Point and bothy

Blimp, Pimple, Tangle cairns

Musselbanks

Big Cairn

A9

Kiltearn

Kiltearn cairns and Slippery Stones

Castlecraig

Balachladdich beach

Foulis Ferry

Sandbanks

Ardullie Point

BLACK ISLE

to Dingwall

1

A Balconie Day

This is the way it was.

A fine July afternoon on the Cromarty Firth, an hour before high water, a little high cloud and a light easterly breeze. At the edge of the water a blue-painted coble is held at anchor, her stern grounded on the beach and her nose pointing into the wind. Where the sea turf meets the pebbles of the beach stands a weatherboard bothy with a tarred felt roof, and sitting on a scaffold-board bench fixed to its west wall are three young men in T-shirts, jeans and rubber thigh boots rolled down at the knee. They are all wearing Polaroid sunglasses. The remains of a meal – sausage and lentil stew – are on the ground beside them, and they have mugs of coffee in their hands. A

The coble. (*ES*)

The bothy. (*RR*)

joint is being passed around, a little red dog is busy licking the plates and two white goats are lying close by in the sun chewing the cud. Not much has happened yet this tide, but all three are keeping their eyes on the water.

The skipper stands up.

'I think I'm getting something well out in the bay.'

They all stand up.

'Yes, that's him. A good heave, too.'

'It looks like he's heading straight in. We'll go down to meet him.'

They put down their mugs, and the first mate takes a last toke on the joint then tosses the roach on the ground, where it is instantly eaten by a goat. They pull up their

The skipper. (*DM*)

The first mate. (*DM*)

The second mate. (*DM*)

boots and walk down to the coble. The second mate picks up the hint rope lying on the beach, the other two throw the loop of anchor rope off its horn, push the coble a few feet out and climb aboard.

The boat men settle to their oars, pull a few strokes out and start to row downwind. The rope man keeps pace with them along the shore. Now the skipper stands up in the bow and scans the water.

'He's still coming in. Give us some rope. We'll get out a bit in case he hits the shore and heads out.'

They pull a few quiet and easy strokes further out.

Now the second mate shouts, 'He's coming along the shore!'

'Pull!'

The second mate starts to pull net off the back of the boat, and the oarsmen go to work, pulling out hard and fast then turning in a tight semi-circle back towards the shore and splashing their oars as they approach the shallows. They jump out, drag the boat's nose up the beach and seize the ends of the net still on the boat. The skipper takes these shorter ropes together in his hands, the other two take a rope each of the longer end.

Rowing the shot. (*RR*)

A net comes in. (*RR*)

'A nice close shot.'

'He should be there.'

'Well ... I think I saw him hit the net.'

They take the net in hand over hand with the ease of long practice, leaning back a little with each pull and letting the slack fall at their feet. Only at the last minute, as the big cork which marks the net's bag comes close to shore, is there any sign of life, a birl in the shallows.

'He's there!'

They crouch low to take the bag in, then drag it up the beach, and there is a slap and clatter of tails on the stones. The skipper runs to the bow of the boat, pulls out the killing sticks and tosses them over. They all kneel on the bag, and the sticks begin to rise and fall. In less than a minute it is all over, and they stand up.

The second mate with a 'donkey'. (*DM*)

'I make it twenty-three.'

'A couple of donkeys, too.'

'Aye, right skipper's fish.'

They pull the net off the catch, pick the fish up and lay them carefully on the beach. The skipper holds up one of the donkeys – a perfect fourteen-pounder – for all to admire. The second mate starts to pull net off the beach into the water, while the other two manoeuvre the boat so that her stern is grounded and facing the net. Then they climb on to the backboard and start to pile the net, one on the ground rope, the other on the floats. They lay the ropes in long strips on the backboard, occasionally pausing to pick up the slack, while the second mate keeps the float rope out to sea and the net coming in smoothly towards them. The beach is clean and there is hardly any weed in the net, but there are some green shore crabs.

The skipper addresses a recalcitrant crab as he disentangles it. 'Come on, Jock, I'm only trying to help you. You wouldn't want to be a cruncher.'

As the bag begins to come in, they pay particular attention, checking for holes, making sure that the net has not rolled around the ground rope, and carefully hanging the big cork over the side so that it will not catch, the next time the net comes off.

Piling the net. (L to R) Doug, Stevie Web, Gary, Robert. (*DM*)

The second mate fetches two wooden boxes from the lean-to behind the bothy and swills them in the water. They pick the fish up – a practised fisher can hold two grilsies in each hand, their tail wrists between the fingers – wash off sand and loose scales and start to pack the boxes. Then, the skipper in the middle, they form a chain and carry the boxes between them up the beach and stack them in the lean-to, covered in wet sacks. Finally, the skipper tows the boat back on station in front of the bothy and hooks the anchor rope on to its horn.

Back on the bench, now passing round a red can of McEwans, the three lean back and take it easy again. Scarcely twenty minutes have passed since the head was spotted.

Fish come up the beach. (*RR*)

2

Catching the Fish

If you asked me what the easiest way is to catch salmon, I'd say set a trap for them in a place where you know there are plenty – a river pool, or the mouth of a river when the fish are running. Your trap does not have to be complicated. The simplest I ever saw was constructed in less than five minutes by a teenage poacher: a few feet of old net wrapped in a U-shaped curtain round four sticks pushed lightly into the sand near the river mouth just before an evening high water. Sure enough, the next morning there was a fish in it. He had swum into the opening of the U, the sticks had collapsed, entangling him in the net, and the tide had receded, leaving him high and dry.

Salmon are such a delicious source of protein, and so easily caught at certain predictable times and places, that as long as there have been people in Scotland they must surely have taken them. We do not know what Scotland's earliest folk called the fish, but it is significant that the word for salmon in some Germanic languages (e.g. German *Lachs*, Swedish *lax*) is derived from an ancient Indo-European word meaning simply 'fish'. This suggests that for these peoples, as Baugh and Cable's *History of the English Language* puts it, 'the salmon was the fish *par excellence.*'

The earliest archaeological evidence we have in Scotland is the remains of a Stone Age fish trap on Coll which operated on exactly the same principle as that teenage poacher's, designed to cut fish off (not just salmon, of course) and leave them stranded as the tide goes out. The first salmon fishers probably concentrated on river pools, which can become crowded with fish when the water is low. Charles St John in his *Wild Sports and Natural History of the Highlands* described an expedition to just such a pool:

> I once fell in with a band of Highlanders, who were engaged in the amusing but illegal pursuit of spearing salmon by torchlight. And a most exciting and interesting proceeding it was. The night was calm and dark. The steep and broken rocks were illuminated in the most brilliant manner by fifteen or sixteen torches which were carried by as many active Highlanders … [standing with spear] ready poised … Then would come loud shouts and a confused hurrying to and fro, as some great fish darted among the men … Every now and then a salmon would be seen hoisted into the air, and quivering on an uplifted spear … Thirty-seven salmon were killed that night.

That was written in the mid-nineteenth century, but I cannot imagine that the technique, known as 'leistering', had changed much since men started using spears ('leisters') and

SPEARING SALMON.

fire. St John's classic work is a remarkable record of Highland wildlife and folk ways before the coming of the railways and the development of organized shooting, stalking and rod-fishing. He was a good naturalist and has many observant things to say about animals and birds, but he was also a dedicated killer. His description of stalking and shooting a great stag ('The Muckle Hart of Benmore') is exciting and has been much anthologized, but he was responsible, almost single-handedly, for exterminating Scotland's then remaining ospreys, by taking their eggs and shooting the parent birds for their skins.

To the Picts, the shadowy folk who inhabited the north and east of Scotland in the first millennium after Christ, salmon were clearly important, perhaps as objects of veneration as well as for

A Pictish salmon.

food. Many of their standing stones, the chief evidence we have of their life, depict salmon – instantly recognizable as such by their adipose fin, that little tag on the back near the tail which only salmonids and a very few other fish possess. In fact, this is not a fin at all, merely a piece of fatty tissue, and we now know that its function is to promote streamlining by reducing turbulence when the fish is swimming at speed.

The firths of the eastern Highlands are full of the remains of traps probably originating even earlier than the Pictish era and designed to catch salmon and other fish. Alistair Stenhouse has studied the yairs (the technical term for these) and has identified ten in the Dornoch Firth, as well as others in the Beauly and Cromarty Firths. A map of 1837 shows many in the Cromarty Firth, and a 1998 survey found a number of yair sites. Essentially, a yair consists of a hook-shaped wall of stone designed to hold fish inside it until the tide goes out and leaves them trapped. The outline of one can be seen off Kiltearn beach, close to our fishing cairns.

Almost as soon as the written record of government begins, it is clear that Scotland's salmon were considered a valuable resource. In the twelfth century King David I declared that all salmon fishing rights belonged to the Crown; loyal servants and institutions such as royal burghs or the church were then rewarded by being granted the right to take fish in specific waters. Our fellow fishers Hamish, Davy and Charlie leased their station in Alness bay from the Crown in the 1980s. And the Kings of Scots also made it clear that salmon were too valuable to be exploited indiscriminately: Alexander II in the thirteenth century decreed that there should be a weekly close time when fishing was not allowed – 'No man sall slay fische fra the Saturday efter the evin song, or evning prayers, untill monday efter the sone rising.'

In 1424, under James I, the first piece of actual legislation regarding salmon was passed, enacting a close season to protect spawning fish; there were harsh penalties for the illegal 'slauchter of Salmonde', and it was decreed that anyone convicted of a third offence should lose his life. Regulations were also enacted to control yairs and cruives. The latter were dam-like structures in rivers designed to trap fish; the Brahan cruives on the Conon were constructed by Napoleonic prisoners of war and caught large numbers of fish until they were removed, by agreement with rod-fishing interests, in 1911, but others remained in use on the Beauly until well after that date. In fact, two basic principles of conservation – annual and weekly close-times, and control of the methods used to catch fish – were firmly established by early modern times. The importance of salmon in these years is underlined by the fact that most laws passed by the Scottish Parliament relating to fishing between 1424 and 1555 mention them; twelve statutes, in fact, regulate salmon fishing exclusively.

It is difficult to assess quite how numerous salmon were in the medieval and early modern periods, but considerable quantities were exported from Scotland. In the late seventeenth century there was a valuable trade between north-east Scotland and France, and the Union of 1707 opened up new markets for salmon in England. It certainly appears that the country produced more than could easily be consumed by its population (under a million until after 1700). And salmon is, in any case, not something you would wish to eat every day; we have all heard the stories, apocryphal though they may be, of apprentices having it written into their contracts of employment that they would not be fed it more than two or three times a week.

Originally, Scottish salmon were exported in barrels, salted; then in the early eighteenth century the more palatable 'Newcastle cure' was introduced – the fish were parboiled and packed in barrels topped up with vinegar. In the late eighteenth century the carriage of fresh fish in ice began, and the remains of icehouses dug into the ground can still be seen at many fishing stations – there is one close to the mouth of the Alness river. Until the railway reached the north (Inverness 1863, Wick 1874), all the fish for export were, of course, carried by boat.

In 1788 the Tay fishery alone employed 2–300 men and was producing some 50–60,000 fish. In 1816, it has been estimated that 300,000 fish were caught in the Tweed. Sweep-netting stations belonging to the Sutherland Estates in the upper Dornoch Firth caught over 20,000 fish in 1833 and over 30,000 in 1834 and 1835. Salmon fisheries were, in fact, an established feature of the Scottish economy. Valuable, too: in 1830 the Spey fishings attracted a yearly rent of £10,714 (at least £1m today). James Thompson in *The Value and Importance of the Scottish Fisheries* (1849) wrote that 'the [value] of the salmon must be very great. In the year 1824 it is supposed that about 200,000 fish reached the metropolis, and in ten years after four and a half millions of lbs, from all sources, a large proportion was from Scotland.' The rateable value of Scottish coastal and river fishings has been estimated (twenty-first century equivalent values) at £4.1m in 1863, increasing to £8.3m by 1892.

A number of different fishing techniques were used: sweep-netting or net and coble (our method) accounted for many fish, but as well as yairs and cruives, there were other styles, some with curious names – stells, cairn nets, pot nets, croy nets, pock nets, haaf nets, scringing (towing a net between two boats). A key moment came with the introduction in the late eighteenth century of a new technique, the stake net. This is a long vertical wall of netting held up by a line of strong wooden poles running at right angles to the shoreline, often several hundred yards long, which interrupts the natural swim of the fish and directs them along it away from the shore and into a series of traps. In the language of salmon fishing, these nets were 'fixed engines', in other words set in one place and then left stationary, as opposed to a sweep net, which is rowed round and keeps moving.

It had long been established that fixed engines were illegal within rivers, with the exception of a few specially licensed cruives like those on the Conon and the Beauly. But stake nets, and the similar fly nets and jumper nets, proved deadly in firths and estuaries (they came to the north-east firths soon after 1800), much to the consternation of the proprietors of river and river-mouth fishings. The owners of valuable fishings in and around the Conon went to court to prevent the use of stake nets by two other proprietors with land adjoining the firth. In 1838 the court found in favour of the plaintiffs, and the estuary was defined as extending as far as the mouth of the firth at the Sutors, inside which the use of fixed nets was prohibited. A number of other court

Stake nets. (*RR*)

cases turned on the question of where a river ends and an estuary begins, but there has always been a good deal of skulduggery of one sort and another associated with salmon fishing, and the decisions of the courts were not always respected; cutting of nets at night was not unknown, and threats were sometimes backed up by firearms.

Rod Richard's research in the Conon Fishery Board's papers has uncovered a number of such incidents, often in solicitors' letters. In 1893, the Patersons were accused of using their pilot's licence as a cover for poaching; Admiralty boats were also suspected of illegal fishing; there was an attempt to prevent the Cromarty fishermen from securing a lease to the Alness fishings, because they were suspected of using it 'for the purpose of disposing of salmon and sea trout caught [presumably illegally] in other waters'. Sometimes the boot was on the other foot: in 1904, the Conon netsmen complained about anglers fishing in tidal waters.

An Act of Parliament in 1828 which imposed an annual close season was the first of a whole series of measures over the nineteenth century – three reports by Special Commissioners, three Parliamentary Select Committee reports and seventeen bills, seven of which became law. By 1900, a mixture of Acts of Parliament, private bills and local regulations created by District Fishery Boards (set up in 1862) had established the following:

- No fixed engines of any sort (yairs or stake nets) permitted in enclosed waters, e.g. the Cromarty Firth inside the Sutors
- Net and coble the only method permitted in rivers and enclosed waters
- Annual close time of at least 168 days (dates varied between districts)
- Weekly close time for all nets of 6.00 pm Saturday to 6.00 am Monday

The weekly close time was known, curiously, as the 'Saturday slap', slapping being the removal of the leader, thus making a fixed engine ineffective. With some revision, for example the Saturday slap moved first to 12.00 midday and then back to 6.00 pm Friday, these were substantially the rules by which we fished.

Some stake nets continued to operate at suitable sites; they could be seen until relatively recently on the beach at Shandwick and at Nairn. But most stations outside the firths and estuaries now fished 'bag nets'; the principle is the same as stake nets, leaders guiding fish into a trap, but instead of being fixed to poles on a beach, the nets are anchored offshore. This was the method used by the many stations along the Tarbat peninsula in Easter Ross: Wilkhaven, Ballone, Rockfield, Tarrel, Geanies, Cadboll, Hilton, Balintore, Port an Righ and Castlecraig.

Something else had changed by 1900. Salmon fishing with a rod had become a popular and fashionable pastime, a part of the gentleman's pilgrimage to the Highlands in August and September to shoot grouse and stalk deer; for the hardier and more dedicated sportsman there might even be a separate trip early in the year, to scrape the ice out of the ferrules of his rod and catch a silver springer. John Buchan's *John Macnab* (1925) set the later fashion for 'doing a Macnab' – shooting a grouse, killing a stag and catching a salmon, all on the same day. In 1863 just 8 per cent of the rateable value of Scotland's salmon fisheries was represented by rod fishing; by 1892 it was 38 per cent, more than either coastal or estuary/fresh water netting.

The laws governing netting in Scotland have always been framed to conserve salmon: in the words of an early statute, so as not to 'destroy the breed of fish, and hurte the common profit of the realme' – deliberately forbidding, for example, all but a less efficient method inside the firths. Rod fishermen have never liked netsmen, but rods and nets need not be in conflict, I believe – I will return to this. By 1900, however, rod fishing interests had begun to lobby for more restrictions on netting, and in response, the Salmon Net Fishing Association of Scotland was founded in 1906.

*   *   *

Our sort of fishing in the firth is with net and coble. This method has probably been practised in some form ever since men learned to make nets – the first reference to it in Scotland is from the Tweed in 1160. Net and coble stations may be in the river,

Net and coble fishing on a blowy day. (*JH*)

at its mouth or in the estuary, and some were worked for many years. The station at Bettyhill, for example, in the mouth of the Naver, was in operation from at least the mid-eighteenth century; we used to stay every year with friends nearby, and I always looked down enviously at the clean, sandy pool where the shot was rowed.

To fish this way you must first have a fishing station. All round the coast of Scotland the right to fish for salmon is owned by someone, often an adjacent landowner, occasionally the Crown or the local river board. In Scots law, this is a 'heritable right'. Often the right is worthless, because few fish come close to the shore at that point. Sometimes it is deadly, as at the mouth of big rivers where fish wait in great numbers when the water is low. But almost no stations are fished now. The rights have been bought out, by angling or conservation bodies, and the stations closed down, or the killing of salmon has been prohibited by Marine Scotland. None of the stations I have worked is being fished today.

To work your station you need a coble. The *Balconie Lady*, our coble for many years, is a wide-bodied, flat-bottomed boat about sixteen feet long, made in Invergordon nearly fifty years ago. She is clinker-built of half-inch larch boards, with two thwarts, each having a pair of iron pins to take nine-foot spruce oars, a backboard across the stern to support the net and a triangle of decking in the bow.

Then you will need a net. Ours is about eighty yards long and eighteen feet deep, the top rope strung with floats and the ground rope weighted with a lead core and

Balconie Lady, full of fish after a good tide. (*DM*)

The net spread for drying and repair. (*RR*)

occasional lead rings to hold it on the bottom. The mesh is by law no smaller than three and a half inches, measured by adding together two sides of a square. The central section of the net is the bag (or 'bosom' as some netsmen call it), a looser sheet of stronger material, marked on the top rope by a triple float and the last part of the net to be dragged in. When I was first at the fishing, Buller used a cotton net, immensely heavy when wet and liable to rot if not regularly dried and aired. Now, of course, it's all nylon. A disaster for fish was the development of monofilament net, which forms an invisible wall and 'gills' them; they swim into it, their heads poke through the mesh and it catches behind their gill covers and entraps them. Then they slowly die. This is now an illegal method of fishing for salmon throughout the British Isles, but it is still occasionally practised, and monofilament is so cheap that unscrupulous fishermen often use hundreds of yards of it; if they are in danger of being caught they simply cut the net free. Then, of course, it may continue to 'ghost fish', catching not only himself (the salmon) but other fish, and entangling diving birds, seals and dolphins. It is a horrible thing.

So you have a fishing station, a boat and a net. But you still need to know how to use them. This is how it works: attached to each end of the net is a length of rope, a hundred feet or so. One end is made fast to the boat, the other is held by a man on the shore. The rope-man stays on shore and two others row the boat out. As they row, the rope-man pulls the net off the back of the boat. The boat describes a semi-circle, net dropping in the water, and returns to shore. With luck, fish are trapped within the semi-circle of net. The two ends of the net are then hauled in, and finally the bag,

A shot in progress. Note the fish jumping inside the net. (*JH*)

where the fish have taken refuge, is pulled ashore, and the fish are killed with a couple of smart cracks on the back of the head. The whole operation takes ten minutes or so.

Sweep-netting as practised in most places is a labour-intensive activity. The standard method is to operate two nets; when one net is pulled in, the other is rowed out and the first one is piled ready for the next shot. It is hard and pretty relentless work, often requiring a winch as well as manpower, and you need a big crew of fit young men; many stations would take on a bunch of students for the season. This rowing the net round time after time and simply trusting to luck we call 'banging' (and I have done it, see Chapter 21, Nigg), but it's not our style. Our fishing is different. Two men can manage it, although three or four are ideal, and since we do not put the net out until we spot fish, the work is not constant; there are long periods for rest, reflection and the craic, in between bursts of activity. Watching the water for fish is ninety per cent of the job, and it is pure pleasure.

A variant of sweep-netting, known as stell-net or cleek-net fishing was once practised on the firth, particularly in our area between Alness and Balconie. One end of the net was secured to the shore and it was run out in a half-circle, but the shot was not completed until fish were seen. Some of the old cairns, the Bell, the Big Cairn and the Slippery Stones, were probably constructed for stell-net, or possibly even stake-net, fishing. In 1904, W. L. Calderwood, Inspector of the Salmon Fisheries of Scotland, described in his report the techniques used in the Cromarty Firth:

> Three forms of net & coble fishing have been distinguished in this area, and two of them have now been put a stop to: *Stell-Net Fishing*, *Lying at Gantry*, and *Fishing with the Long Rope*, and it may be said that each is an attempt to reduce the labour of fishing and to secure a greater certainty of success.

In other words, these techniques were aimed at reducing the hard work involved in continuous 'banging'. The first two involved running net out and then halting the shot, sometimes by anchoring the boat, until fish were seen. This is the 'toot and haul' method occasionally employed by Buller on a misty morning (see Chapter 11, Early Days).

However, since these two methods involved the net lying stationary in the water, Calderwood reports that it 'must be regarded as a fixed engine and therefore illegal within an estuary.' He continues:

> [These have], therefore, been stopped, and *Fishing with the Long Rope* resorted to. This is again a method to get over a preliminary operation in making the shot, the benefit being not only to save time but to allow those in the boat to occupy a position from which they can successfully watch for fish. At the same time there is the advantage that the labour of making repeated unsuccessful hauls of the net is saved … the rope or 'tow' is paid out from the boat, which is then anchored and the shot stopped before any of the net is drawn off into the water. In this way no

actual fishing appliance is kept in the water, nor, it may be said, is there any very apparent obstruction to the passage of fish. On these grounds, I am informed, the District Fishery Board have decided that no real objection can be taken to the operation.

This is a precise description of the way that Buller's grandfather fished – indeed, he was probably at it when Calderwood wrote his report – and lying off in the boat on the Long Rope watching for fish is just the way we do it, too.

Some years ago, a new head bailiff was appointed locally. It was a grey, rather misty morning, and we were fishing on the Little Bell, lying off in the boat minding our own business and watching the water, when we heard the sound of an outboard in the distance. Out of the mist emerged a RIB with three men in it, going at top speed. About twenty yards away, the boat executed a tight turn, sending out a wash which completely spoiled the sight on the water, cut the power and drifted towards us. An awkward exchange ensued.

'What are you doing here?'

'We're fishing.'

'And what's this?'

The boat had now drifted toward our rope, and the bailiff reached out to it with a boathook. He was clearly expecting to find net underneath it, but when he lifted it, his face fell. This was not stell-net fishing, let alone lying at gantry. We were perfectly legal long-rope men, and there was nothing he could do about it. We were not bothered again that season, or for many seasons to come.

Long-rope men. Eddie and self in the boat, Oz on the cairn. (*JH*)

3

An Alness Day

Back in the day again, at a different sort of place.

A pale grey July morning, with a hint of warmth in the light south-westerly breeze. 'A fine dull day', says Buller, perfect for the job, and the fish are running. Low water is still a couple of hours away. Out in the channel there is plenty jumping, sometimes two at once, and a good head has already gone past, putting up a big heave but out of reach in the deep.

On Teaninich cairn. A wet day, looking towards the Yankee pier and a parked oil rig. (*RR*)

On Teaninich cairn three men and a boy in oilskin jackets stand in front of a stack of fish boxes as tall as they are. In the big grey coble, anchored sixty feet off and connected to the cairn by the hint rope, Buller watches the water from the bow with an oilskin over his shoulders; his mate sits on the stern thwart. Behind the cairn, fifty yards up the shore on the seaweed and stones of the ebb, is the grey Fergie tractor and boat trailer. Everyone is looking east, towards the end of the Yankee Pier.

A shout from Buller, and much pointing on the cairn. Buller shrugs off his jacket, lifts the anchor and he and the mate take hold of their oars. Someone on the cairn picks up the rope, and a warning shout comes from the boat: 'Don't pull! Give us rope!' They row out a few strokes, Buller in a half crouch and scanning the water intently.

'He's coming on … pull!'

The net comes off smoothly in a semi-circle as they row round the head and back to the cairn. Buller tosses the anchor out, while his mate lifts the back oars off their pins and manoeuvres the boat in readiness to re-pile the net. Buller stands back now and lets the crew do the work of pulling the net in. They know the job, after all. It's immediately obvious that this is going to be a big shot. There's a lot of activity – birls at the float rope and a couple of jumps inside the net.

'Keep your hands low', Buller warns the men on the ground ropes, then, 'Don't bother about him', as the boy on one float rope pauses to attend to a grilsie gilled in the side netting.

Now the bag is approaching the cairn, and there are more birls in the shallows as fish start to panic. Finally, all four bend down, seize the ropes around the bag and drag it with difficulty up on to dry land, where there is a furious thrashing and spattering of tails on the stones. The mate reaches into the bow of the coble, picks up four killing sticks – it's crucial not to touch these before the fish are landed – and throws them to the crew. One of the sticks is a candy-twist chair leg of oak, the others are eighteen-inch lengths of blackthorn.

The crew kneel on the bag and go to work with the sticks. A couple of sharp taps do for each fish, well down the nose so as not to bruise the shoulder meat. Finally, all are quiet and the crew stand up. The boy, excited, starts to count them, but Buller tells him, 'Plenty time for that when you box them. We'll need to get this net back on – there's fish about, the day.'

Now Buller himself goes into action, picking up the ground rope and climbing on to the backboard of the coble, where he and the first mate stand to pile the net. Pulling is only semi-skilled work, but this is important – a clumsily piled net could easily come off in a lump and spoil the next shot.

Two of the crew work on the net, one standing in the water and keeping the float rope out to sea, the other sorting the ground rope so that it comes smoothly to hand. The rest pick the fish off the net and box them – about a dozen to each flat wooden box – then swill the boxes in the sea before stacking them on the cairn. It's a pretty good shot – fifty-four – but not exceptional for the station. The best shot here has been in three figures, and a good tide at this time of year should see seven or eight boxes,

Piling the net. Buller (second left), Doug next to him, Paul far right. Oil rigs and the Sutors in the background. (*RR*)

around a hundred fish. This time they are all grilse – nothing over about 6lbs, and a lot of them 'Alness eels', slim fellows of just 3lbs or 4lbs.

It takes only a few minutes to load the net, then Buller and the mate step off the backboard, put the oars back on and turn the boat's nose into the wind. They are about to climb aboard and head back out to their station, when Paul the Pole pipes up from the cairn:

'Look, ovair!'

Paul has been in Scotland since the war, but 'over' is still just about his only preposition ('Feesh commink ovair!'), and now it is to draw attention to the flat half-bottle he has taken out of his piece-bag. He works in the distillery, and this will be a dram worth waiting for, but Buller keeps a close eye on the water while the bottle goes round.

Paul with enough grilse to fill a box.

Teaninich cairn at dawn, with the Yankee pier and the aluminium smelter chimneys in the background. (*RR*)

4

Himself

The one thing most people know about salmon is that they return from the sea to swim up the rivers they were born in, jumping dramatically when they come to waterfalls and weirs. Beyond that, there's a good deal of vagueness, usually padded out with half-remembered footage from TV nature programmes about bears catching salmon in North America. The fish those bears feed on are Pacific salmon, one of several species related to our quarry, the Atlantic salmon (*Salmo salar*); they are by no means as good to eat (the 'wild salmon' for sale in supermarkets nowadays is probably Alaskan sockeye), and they are different in another way, too – after spawning, all Pacific salmon die (they are, as the scientific term has it, 'semelparous'), whereas their Atlantic cousins can survive to breed again, even twice more.

Unlike eels, which spawn in the sea and return to fresh water to mature, salmon breed in rivers and do their growing at sea. They are said to be 'anadromous', running up rivers, as opposed to the 'catadromous' eels. They can enter their river in virtually any month of the year, but most arrive in spring and summer. Spawning happens, however, in the dog days of winter, so fish which entered the river early in the year ('springers') will have spent many months in fresh water, whereas autumn fish may run straight up and spawn almost immediately.

Grossly simplified, this is how the life cycle of the Atlantic salmon plays out. The hen fish lay their eggs in 'redds', furrows which they cut into gravel (they prefer it to be fairly coarse) in the well oxygenated headwaters of the river of their birth or in its tributary burns. The eggs hatch in spring, and the tiny creatures which emerge, still with a yolk sac attached, are known as alevins. These remain in the gravel, safe from predators, feeding on the yolk. Once they have digested it all they begin to work their way up until they are swimming free. At this stage, about an inch long, they are known as fry, and although they start to feed on insects and their larvae, they themselves are pretty near the bottom of the food chain and prey for trout, herons, mergansers, kingfishers, even dippers. Many species of fish lay eggs which just float free in the water. Salmon (and trout) at least give their eggs the protection of a redd, although many are lost or eaten by predators (including their own young) in the confusion of spawning. But given the inevitable mortality rate between egg and adult, it is just as well that a hen salmon lays almost a thousand eggs for every pound of her body weight.

By early summer the fry will have moved into the main flow of their river and grown to become parr – several inches long and rather like little trout, but with a more streamlined shape and deeply forked tail, their gill covers less spotted and not

Parr.

extending back past the line of the eye. Rod fishermen will be familiar with them, because they readily take a fly. Extraordinarily, cock fish become sexually mature at this stage and many take part in the spawning frenzy at the end of the year. They will eat any eggs that float loose, of course, but they also position themselves to fertilize eggs laid by the mature females. They can ejaculate only a small quantity of milt (sperm), but because they hover so close to the hen's vent, unnoticed by the big cocks who often spill their seed carelessly, it has been estimated that as many as a quarter of all fish may be fathered by parr.

After two or three years in the river – the length of time depends on water temperature and availability of food – parr undergo a physiological change in preparation for going to sea: the level of guanine in their skin increases, and their spotted appearance, perfect camouflage for a river life, changes to a silvery look, better protective colouring in the ocean. At this stage they are known as smolts, and they are the lucky ones; perhaps as few as one in a hundred eggs reach the smolt stage.

In spring the smolts gather, now about six inches long, and move downstream. In early May, fishing the cairns at the mouth of the Alness, we sometimes saw them, a crowd of little silver fish jumping for joy as they hit the firth. It is not easy for a fish that has grown up in fresh water to adapt to the sea, but smolts manage it by moving gradually into salt water and excreting excess salt through specialized cells in their gills, gut and kidneys. Now strictly speaking classed as 'post-smolts', they set off in shoals on the long journey to their feeding grounds in the North Atlantic. This coincides with the spring plankton bloom in the ocean, just the time when the shrimps and fry on which they feed become available in large quantities.

A good deal of research is currently being undertaken to track the movements of smolts at sea, but as with much of the salmon's marine life, a lot remains a mystery. The smolts will take a month or two to reach an area of sea, somewhere off Iceland, Greenland or the Faroe Islands, where the Arctic and Atlantic waters meet and where deep water rich in nutrients comes to the surface, and here they begin to feed in earnest. Salmon are fast, agile, powerful fish and will eat anything they can catch, but one food in particular is important – krill, the small shrimp-like crustaceans which live in the open ocean. It is astaxanthin, a carotenoid pigment in these, which gives the flesh of the salmon its pinkness – salmon farmers add it to the feed, otherwise their fish would be an unappealing grey/white colour.

The chief reason why salmon are farmed so successfully is their ability to grow incredibly fast. A smolt which leaves the river weighing, say, 4oz can return after just

A smolt. Remarkable to think that this little fish could grow to weigh 8lbs in just 15 months at sea. (*Ness District Salmon Fishery Board*)

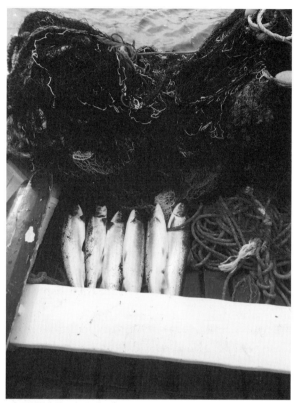

A catch of grilsies.

fifteen months at sea weighing 8lbs. Fish returning after one winter at sea (1SW in the jargon) are known as grilse. These can weigh anything from around 2lbs – a very small grilse, admittedly, but I have seen them this size, small enough to be taken by an osprey – to 10lbs or even more, if they return late in the year. In practice, we refer to any fish under about 8lbs as 'a grilsie' – netsmen don't go in for scale analysis, which is, like examining the rings of a tree, the only reliable way to tell a fish's age.

Some fish remain in the sea for more than one season; those which spend two, three or sometimes even more winters at sea are consequently bigger when they return, generally early or late in the year, as opposed to the grilse which mostly appear from late June to early August. The size of the very biggest fish is often a matter of hearsay, fable or outright lies. A few years ago, I edited Volumes I and II of *The Domesday Book of Giant Salmon* (Constable, 2007, 2010), splendid publications full of pictures of enormous fish and descriptions of their capture – real fisherman's pornography, in fact. Its author, Fred Buller, a well known writer on fishing and a very experienced salmon angler, collected records of all the salmon over 50lbs in weight caught by any method in fresh and salt water on both sides of the Atlantic since the beginning of the nineteenth century. There are just 553 of them, mostly between 50lbs and 60lbs. Of course, he will have missed some, and other big fish must have gone completely unrecorded, but the relatively small total suggests that seriously big fish are pretty rare. There are just three reasonably well attested records of fish over 100lbs: one of 103lbs (River Forth) and another of 109lbs (River Hope), both captured by poachers, and a fish of 102lbs 8oz netted legally in the River Nemen in Lithuania.

Incidentally, when I had the pleasure of meeting Fred Buller I asked him what he thought about 'catch and release' on salmon rivers, then beginning to be common practice. He looked at me conspiratorially and said, 'Man is a predator. I don't put fish back.' This sentiment was echoed by another experienced rod fisherman of my acquaintance, who recently declared, 'If I was allowed, I would bang every fresh male grilse on the head without question.'

Very few young fish survive their river life to go to sea, and their migration itself is a hazardous undertaking. But mature fish are programmed to return to the river of their birth for a very good reason: if you have survived to return and spawn, it makes sense to give your offspring the same chances in life. It is still not completely understood how fish find their way back to their own river. Once they approach the coast they can recognize the smell, or taste, of their own water – one study has found that they can detect this at just one part per 80 billion – but how do they know the way back from the feeding grounds? Memory of some sort may be involved, and it has recently been suggested that they navigate by sensing the earth's magnetic field. Rather than run straight into their river, and experience the physiological shock of a rapid change from salt to fresh

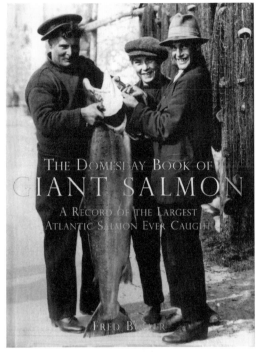

The Domesday Book. Netsmen from Counterfeit Sands at the mouth of the River Exe with a 61¼lb fish, 18 March 1924.

water, most fish spend some time in the brackish water of an estuary. When they do enter the river, their problem is not how to get rid of salt but how to retain the salt their bodies need, but once again their kidney and gill functions adapt successfully.

Once in fresh water, fish may snap at a passing worm or a fisherman's lure, much as you and I would snack on a bowl of peanuts, but they cease to eat regularly – in any case, most salmon rivers do not contain enough food to sustain fish of their size, and they are carrying all the fat accumulated in the rich feeding at sea. Then their bodies begin to change. They lose their silver sheen, and any parasitic sea lice they are carrying drop off. We sometimes get fish in the net which have 'a touch of colour in them' and have clearly been in the river and come out again. Readers of Henry Williamson's *Salar the Salmon*, an unrivalled telling of the fish's life story, will recall that Salar, his hero, runs back down to the sea for a while after suffering the trauma of being hooked, played and lost by an angler. He also escapes from sweep-netters in the estuary when a 'pug' (a big sea trout) breaks through the net. Fish sometimes spend time in rivers other than their own. A recent study surprisingly found that almost half of the fish which entered the rivers of the Cromarty Firth dropped back to the estuary and ascended an adjacent river after several weeks of freshwater residence.

In the river, the hen fish turn from silver to a dull pewter colour, with a touch of copper and some spots, but the cocks change more dramatically. They go a deep red and orange (becoming 'tartan soldiers') and develop a massively hooked lower jaw, or

A ripe cock fish, from Bloch, *Ichtylogie* (1785–97).

'kype', for fighting with rivals. As the water turns colder, they all move upriver towards the spawning areas. When the time comes, the hen fish turns on her side and thrashes up and down to part the gravel and create a redd, while the cocks hover around her, fighting each other for the opportunity to fertilize her eggs. Once the act has taken place, the hen covers the eggs with gravel again.

Fish that have finished spawning are called kelts, and rather more than 90 per cent of them will not survive to spawn again. A good many die in the river – their bodies a feast for the gulls and crows, as well as a gift of nutrients to the river of their birth – and others drop back down to the sea but are so weakened that they do not survive. The small number which remain in the river and recover are known as 'well mended kelts'. These rapidly become silver again and, unsurprisingly, are ravenously hungry; consequently, rod fishermen quite often catch them. I once had one myself, on the Alness in early April. Apart from being a bit thin, it looked for all the world like a fresh fish. Then we tried to eat it … the flesh was so pale and tasteless that even the cat turned up its nose.

The fish that run the rivers of the Cromarty Firth are not big – of the thousands I have caught none has reached 30lbs – nor are they deep in the body. They have a definite 'family' look, whichever river of the firth they belong to. Occasionally we get a fish which looks completely different, shorter and thicker, perhaps from the Beauly, the Ness, the Nairn or one of the Dornoch Firth rivers. Catching a big fish – anything over about 12lbs is a 'donkey' – is always an occasion. Our typical fish is a slim 5lb or 6lb grilse, and many are smaller, little eel-like things of just 3lbs or 4lbs. I recorded the average size of fish we caught over a number of seasons, and this varied from just over 6lbs to almost 8lbs. Their sides are always silver and their bellies pale, but their backs vary from olive green to brown to dark blue or almost black. Many carry sea lice around the tail and the vent, showing that they are fresh from the ocean. Now and again we get a fish which is so perfect that we lay him out in the boat or on the cairn to admire, but usually we just slide them into the stern and get on with piling the net for the next shot.

People sometimes ask what I feel about the many fish lives I have taken. Not much, is my answer. Once upon a time I caught them for a living, and latterly we took very few. And it is a humane way to take them. A fish caught by us does not know the slow death of the gill net or the bag net's long confinement, let alone the painful struggle up and down a pool of the fish caught on rod and line. Instead, a sweep-netted fish experiences just a few minutes of confusion and a few seconds of panic, before oblivion descends. We always treat our catch with respect. I cannot bear the sight of a fish left to gasp its life out; we aim to kill them as quickly and efficiently as possible, and at the end of the season long ago we would always make a point of lifting the ground rope and letting one go free, a kind of offering to the piscine gods.

I have a real problem with catch and release, as now practised almost universally by rod fishermen. Shooting game birds or stalking deer, you look for as clean and quick a kill as possible. Rod fishing is the only sport where the more your quarry struggles

'Oblivion descends'. The skipper kills a good fish. (*RR*)

(anglers call it 'playing', though there's not much fun in it for the fish) the more you enjoy it. And then, at the end of it all, you don't even eat the poor thing. Marine Scotland, the body charged with protecting Scotland's coastal waters, estimates that some 10 per cent of fish do not survive being caught and released, and I wouldn't be surprised if the mortality rate is even higher.

Anything we catch is destined for the pot, at home or away. With bigger fish – say, 12lbs and over – smoking is the best way; the rather coarse flakes of flesh in a big fish are not particularly appetizing, however magnificent it may look served up with cucumber slices along its lateral line and a lemon in its mouth. A fish for smoking wants to be at least 8lbs. Anything much less, and the 'side' (half a fish) is too thin and may become dry; the process of gutting, filleting and smoking will reduce the weight of a fish by about a third. As a fish for the table, we look for a small but fat grilse, something around 4–5lbs. It is bad luck to sell the first fish of the season, so this is always cut up and distributed among the crew. My preference then is to slice my piece into steaks, roll them in seasoned flour and fry them in butter. Actually, I am not that fond of salmon. Given good mayonnaise, a classic poached fish eaten cold is very acceptable – as long as I'm the one in charge and have thoroughly scaled and de-finned it before cooking, then removed all the skin, the cartilage and the grey subcutaneous fat. I'm fussy. I have never forgotten being asked out to dinner one Saturday night in the middle of the season; it had been a busy week – fish, fish, fish every day – and I was looking forward to a quiet weekend away from it all, but our kind hostess, no cook, not only served us salmon but dished it up skin-on and half raw.

At the bothy we would often barbecue a fish – gutted and scaled, head and tail off, wrapped in well-oiled silver foil or put in a wire cage, and set over a driftwood fire. Perhaps the finest method of all was Doug's, which he would lay on for the end-of-season bothy party. First, he got a good fire going in the barbecue pit dug into the beach and lined with big stones. He took a whole fish, not scaled or gutted, and wrapped it in many layers of wet newspaper, then an even thicker layer of bracken, and tied up the bundle, by now several times the size of the fish itself, with netting twine. Once the fire had a good heart to it he raked the embers aside, laid the fish on the hot stones and piled fuel back on top of it. After 45 minutes or so – depending on the size of the fish – he levered out with an old tattie graip something that looked for all the world like a charred log and laid it on a fish-box lid. With a sharp knife he cut into the covering, and bracken, newspaper and fish skin all peeled off neatly. The newspaper, the bracken and the guts inside the fish keep the flesh moist, and the flavour is an exquisite mix of barbecue and smoke.

When I started fishing, and well into the 1980s, our fish were smoked by Steve Fraser at Englishton, above the old road to Inverness near Bunchrew. Steve was a veteran of Bomber Command (I think he was a navigator); he had been shot down over France and taken in by a French family, with whom he kept in touch and often visited. You could tell you were nearing his place when you saw the crowd of gulls wheeling over one of his fields. Just far enough from his house to keep the smell at bay,

On the barbecue. (*DM*)

here was the pit into which he threw the heads, tails and guts of the fish he smoked – many hundreds every year, so the birds were performing a crucial scavenging service, although he occasionally shovelled some earth on top of the remains. Steve's operation was housed in a squarely functional breeze-block building. This held his big electric smoker – electric in the sense that this supplied the heat; the actual smoke came, of course, from woodchips and sawdust, mostly oak, although every smoker has his own mixture, the secret of which is never divulged. Inside the building, which also served as his office, there was a wonderful aroma of woodsmoke with a hint of fish at the back of it, and everything in the place was smoked: the table at which he sat, the Ness Motors calendar on the wall, the kettle on the shelf. His telephone, once white, was a particularly rich shade of mahogany.

Steve loved a gossip and was a fund of information about fish and fishing. Anglers brought their fish to him – these were the days before 'catch and release' – so he knew the rivers of the Highlands; and netsmen did too, so he knew who was catching what. One of the puzzles of salmon angling is why fish take a fly or a lure in the river, when in theory they have stopped feeding once they approach fresh water. I once asked Steve whether he had ever found food (I never have) in the stomachs of the many thousands of fish he had gutted over the years. Only once, he said, in a very dry summer, when a batch of fish from the Beauly Firth had sand eels in them. His theory, and I'm sure he was right, was that the fish had got tired of hanging around in the firth waiting for a spate and had swum back into the outer Moray Firth and started feeding again.

Steve's product was superb. He had built up a wealth of experience over the years, yet his operation was small enough to give the fish his personal attention and adapt the process according to all sorts of variables – size of fish, ambient temperature, customer's preferences, and so on. He knew that I liked a fairly light smoke, for instance. Smoked salmon, now a byword for luxury, must once have been a staple food to see many Highlanders through the winter, and it would then have been very heavily salted and smoked, more like a kipper than the familiar delicate pink slices on brown bread of today. Did Steve eat much of his own product, I once asked him. Not much, he said, and only one very special part of the side, about a third of the way up from the tail. I knew exactly the bit he meant; it is indeed special – smooth in texture and particularly rich in taste. Salmon farming was getting going in Steve's later years, but he refused to smoke farmed fish; he didn't like handling them, scornful of the flabby texture of their flesh.

People often find their first taste of smoked salmon disappointing – dry, salty, oily, or sometimes all three. There is, of course, a lot of inferior stuff out there, almost all of it farmed fish nowadays and smoked on an industrial scale. But it's also a question of how it is treated once smoked. This is my way with a side:

Lay your side out on newspaper, skin side down, and have to hand a razor-sharp ham knife (long, narrow and whippy), a pliers and a plate for the slices.

Trim the side, cutting a thin strip off the edge all the way round (this will be mostly fat and cartilage) then take a first thin slice off the top (this is quite dry). If you are feeling prodigal you can wrap all this up in a sheet of the newspaper and bin it. Or you can keep it to make pâté. Or you can give it to the cat, if you have a cat who likes fish – Sid, our ginger tom, used to come running into the kitchen as soon as he heard me sharpening the knife.

Now you are into the good stuff. Lay the knife flat on the side and work it from tail to head with a slight sawing motion. Aim to cut your slices about 2mm thick. You may come up against a row of pin bones; these will be revealed by your first slice, and you should use the pliers to pull them out before you cut any further.

Keep slicing, cutting away as you go any discoloured flesh or grotty bits near the edges of the side. Stop when the flesh starts to change colour and to become a bit oily. You are now near the skin, and you can scrape off these last bits and bin, pâté or cat them.

Serve with the brown bread of your choice, cut quite thick and buttered, a good squeeze of lemon and black pepper.

Some people might think this method wasteful, but probably no more than a tenth of the side fails to reach the plate, and those are the bits which spoil the pure, heavenly taste of the real thing – smoky, almost meaty and, if the smoke has been a very light one, with the faintest delightful hint of decay. The crucial thing is to have plenty of it – fairly thick slices on chunky bread and butter, none of your tiny triangles topped with wafer-thin pieces.

If you are ambitious, you might like to try making your own *gravadlax*. Here's Kim's recipe:

1kg middle cut of fish
50g flaked sea salt or semi-coarse rock salt
100g white sugar
1 tsp ground white pepper
1 generous bunch fresh dill, coarsely chopped

Fillet the fish, leaving the skin on. Use tweezers/small pliers or fingers to remove any pin-bones.

Mix salt, sugar and pepper and spread evenly over both fillets, followed by the chopped dill.

Place the fillets together, flesh to flesh, and wrap well in foil, then lay in a tray with sides (the liquefying salt and sugar may leak).

Put in the fridge with a weight (around 1kg) on top. Leave for 48 hours, turning twice, then unwrap, scrape away any salt, dill and liquid.

Slice and serve with lemon, or with a sauce of 50/50 mayonnaise and plain yoghurt, flavoured with capers, lemon and dill, or with a mustard sauce.

If you have a whole fish available, and a very cool place in which to store it, you could try a more basic, homespun method: use whole sides of fish and scale up the amounts of salt, sugar, pepper and dill. Wrap the fish not in foil but in fresh pine branches and weigh them down with something seriously heavy – breeze-blocks are ideal.

Before Steve Fraser retired, Doug took lessons from him and set up in business himself. Very soon, he was producing fish as good as Steve's or, dare I say it, sometimes even better. Doug's smokehouse was a strictly homemade affair, down by the burn behind his house. It looked for all the world like a large outdoor khazi, and of course it did not have the capacity of Steve's professional kiln, but the product was superb. A concrete floor for the fire,

Doug in his smokehouse. (*FC*)

with racks above to hang the fish (he could take a couple of dozen sides at a time) and an adjustable air intake and chimney; next door, space to gut and fillet the fish and a big table on which to lay the sides in salt. The basic procedure is simple enough: the sides lie in coarse salt, sometimes with added sugar, for about 24 hours, then hang in smoke for a further day. The trick is to adjust your timing according to the prevailing wind and temperature. Then there is the choice of wood. True to the smoker's creed, Doug never revealed his exact recipe, but I know it was based on oak with the addition of a little softwood, and fruitwood if he could get it.

Good though the best smoked fish is, the finest eating of all, far better than himself in my view, are sea trout. In the last few years of fishing we caught very few, perhaps simply because the net was not going out that often, but before that they appeared pretty regularly. Occasionally these were finnock, under a pound in weight, although fish this size usually found a way to escape through the net. Just once, at Kiltearn, we caught a fish of over 3lbs, although we had better ones at Nigg (see Chapter 21). But the standard trootie was somewhere in the 1½–2lb class. Occasionally, when nothing else was happening but trout were jumping, we would row a shot specifically for them. This hardly ever succeeded; virtually all the trout we caught were 'by-catch' in shots for fish. I can only recall one really successful trout shot, on the Balconie bank: they were going mad at a shoal of sprats close in to the shore, we got round them and pulled

Three good sea trout in the catch. (*JH*)

in about a dozen. Steve K and Rik had an even better shot at Alness one day, about thirty, I think.

Sea trout are simply brown trout who have adopted a sea-going lifestyle. Both are *Salmo trutta*. Like himself, sea trout spawn in the river, often many times, but do most of their feeding and growing in salt water; the trout we caught were usually full of sand eels and shrimps. Trout which live in fresh water will occasionally take it into their head to go to sea, and then there is an intermediate form – sometimes known as 'slob' trout – which inhabit the brackish water of river mouths and estuaries. We used to catch these sometimes at the mouth of the Black Rock. Were they brown trout? Were they sea trout? It was impossible to tell. In any case, sea trout do not make the long ocean voyages of their cousin *Salmo salar*, but stay in coastal waters. This doesn't mean they can't grow big. The British record is not far off 30lbs, although it has recently been disputed on the grounds that the fish may have been a salmon/sea trout hybrid – a reminder of how closely the two salmonids are related. Indeed, sea trout are often miscalled 'salmon trout' by fishmongers and restaurateurs. The large trout we caught at Nigg, fish probably belonging to the Ness or the Beauly, were not always easy to tell from grilse of the same weight, but they are spottier and – another reliable way of telling – their mouths extend back beyond a vertical line drawn down from the eye.

Sea trout are much warier than salmon. Whereas the latter are just passing through the firth, driven by the imperative to run the river and breed, the trout are residents and know the territory. Unless the water is very calm or the shot is rowed very clumsily, it is remarkably rare for salmon to dive deep or take evasive action; sea trout always do. At Nigg, where we caught plenty, they always attempted to get through the net, frequently gilling themselves in the process (the mesh was 4½″, as opposed to the 3½″ of the regular nets). And it was noticeable that Henry, the seal, shared my preference for trout and made a beeline for them, whereas he would often leave a gilled grilsie alone. I once watched a seal pursue a trout right into the shallows on the Foulis beach; he was half out of the water by the time he grabbed it.

Our way with a sea trout caught on the Balconie beach was simple. As soon as the net is piled and ready for the next shot, take your knife and scale, de-fin, gut and fillet the fish. Roll the fillets in seasoned oatmeal and fry them in a mixture of sunflower oil and butter. Aim to take your first mouthful no more than half an hour after the fish was swimming. Oz reminded me, not long before he died, of a glorious sea trout we ate together at Balconie on 7 June 1977. I know the exact day, because it was the Queen's Silver Jubilee, and Oz, no monarchist, had made his way to the shore to escape the local orgies of patriotism. Oz shared my pernickety taste in fish – no bones, no fins, no scales, no skin – and he appreciated the clean way we filleted it.

In 2005 SEPA (the Scottish Environmental Protection Agency) carried out surveys of the fish populations in the Cromarty Firth using a combination of beam trawls, fyke netting (traps) and seine netting and recorded the following species: plaice, cod, saithe, lesser pipefish, three-spined stickleback, eelpout, pollack, herring, goby, whiting, butterfish, juvenile flatfish, great pipefish, sea trout and flounder. Some of these we have never seen in the net, probably because they do not occur far up the firth, but as well as himself (*Salmo salar*) and his cousin the sea trout (*Salmo trutta*), a number of other fish do turn up from time to time. Of course, with a mesh size of 3½″, the net will get round many smaller fish and fry which escape, the sticklebacks, for example, which live in brackish water near the river mouth. The following list is as complete as my memory allows:

Grey mullet (*Crenimugil lubrosus*) These were common at one time (my diary records days when we caught a couple of dozen) and are very good eating provided they are thoroughly scaled and cleaned, scraping away the black lining of the stomach cavity and taking care to avoid the brutally sharp dorsal fin. They are also excellent hot-smoked – I used a little Abu smoker. It is over twenty years since we caught one, but they were even a nuisance once, because they put up a swim rather like himself; the shake is somewhat faster, but difficult to ignore since it might be fish, so we quite often ended up having a shot of them. Unlike himself, they will readily jump out of the net as it approaches the shore. Buller used to fish for them in Alness bay and would take along a bag of chaff or sawdust to sprinkle on the surface of the water inside the net and stop them jumping.

Bass (*Dicentrarchus labrax*) A very occasional small one caught at Alness.

Mackerel (*Scomber scombrus*) Late in the season we sometimes see big shoals of mackerel making a shimmer on the surface, but I only saw one caught, at Kiltearn.

Flounder (*Platichthys flesus*) Known as 'flukes' or 'flukies' and a frequent catch. Mostly under 1lb, although Dave J caught one of almost 3lbs on the Old Wife bank in the middle of the firth. Delicious fried for breakfast, if really fresh.

Plaice (*Pleuronectes platessa*) Infrequent, and known to us, thanks to Kim, as *Rödspätta*.

Common Skate (*Dipturus batis*) Just one, caught on the Balconie bank. My diary says, 'Ate the skate. Disgusting.'

Monkfish (*Lophius piscatorius*) These hideous fish are known to us, courtesy of Stevie Web, by the wonderfully apt Caithness name of 'cudplucker'. Caught fairly often by their huge heads, but their bodies always too small to be worth eating.

Lesser pipefish (*Syngnathus rostellatus*) Could easily get through the net, but their long bodies sometimes get across the mesh, and they are not lively enough to extricate themselves.

Sprat (*Sprattus sprattus*) The possessor of a splendid Latin name, and of course far too small to stay in the net, but occasionally present in such numbers that some get caught.

Then there are the invertebrates:

Shore crab (*Carcinas maenas*) Very few shots do not contain a crab or two. They delay the process of piling the net because they have to be removed; even a dead crab's claw can cause a tack in the net which could spoil the next shot.

Edible crab (*Cancer pagurus*) Generally known in Scotland as 'partans', and although common further down the firth (a pal caught plenty in pots laid out along the Invergordon pier, and we got them regularly at Nigg), appear very rarely even as far east as Alness.

Common starfish (*Asterias rubens*) Sometimes present in large numbers, especially on the biggest tides.

Mussels (*Mytilus edulis*) and **Common Whelks** (*Buccinum undatum*) Both are often dragged up by the net. Old Paul used sometimes to collect the whelks and take a bagful home to boil for his tea. I tried them once, and once only – rubber with a faint hint of fish. Occasionally we would see winkle-pickers at work along the shore, filling their string sacks. One week, I spotted an advertisement in the *Ross-shire Journal*: 'Large winkles wanted. Phone Brenda', and a phone number. My seaside-postcard sense of humour was tickled, and I sent it to *Private Eye*. They didn't print it.

The local mussels are not much good, either. Even the bigger ones contain disappointingly little meat, and too much untreated sewage gets into the rivers for us to be happy about eating a filter feeder.

Moon jellyfish (*Aurelia aurita*) Very common, especially in warm weather, and occasionally present in such numbers as to weigh down the net.

Lion's mane jellyfish (*Cyanea capillata*) Known to us as 'scalders'. Large, disgusting in appearance and difficult to extract from the net without getting stung – even a fragment of tentacle will give you a sting rather like a nettle.

5

Going Solo

When you have a shot, there are four ropes to pull – a ground rope and a float rope on each wing of the net – so the ideal crew is four. Just occasionally, on a really big day when the fish are coming thick and fast, a few more can be helpful. A couple of extra hands can begin piling the net as soon as it starts to come in, for example. There were days when we had half a dozen or more in the crew. In practice, however, we most often fished as a threesome, which is fine as long as

A big crew, the net being piled as it comes in. (*ES*)

One man and his boat. (*RR*)

everyone knows the job. Novices can be a trial. Sometimes they start taking net off the boat before the skipper shouts, 'Pull!' Sometimes they don't pull hard enough and fish escape under the rope. They get excited and make a lot of noise, they get bored and want to go home, or they ask silly questions.

Just occasionally, a fisher may have a shot on his own. I have done it twice, both times at Balconie. The first was in the second half of August, towards the end of a good season. Low water was about 8.00 am and the weather was fine and calm. I got to the bothy in good time and made a piece and a flask. I can't remember who the crew for the day was, but nobody showed. No mobile phones in these days, of course, to stir them up. But the water was calm and the weather was set fair; it was a perfect morning for the sandbank and I decided to go it alone. If anyone did appear, they could just walk out. I wasn't really bothered – we had caught enough fish that year.

The one thing I knew I needed was an anchor for the hint rope, so I took along a big metal ground screw, some three feet long, which was lying at the back of the bothy. There were a few of these in the Estate sheds, and somebody told me once that they were relics of the Great War, used to fix barbed wire in front of the trenches. Launching the boat was going to be a little tricky on my own, but I tied a length of rope between her bow ring and the tow bar of the tractor; when I reached the mouth of the river I backed the trailer in until the boat started to float, then hopped off the tractor, pulled her free, unhitched the rope, threw out the anchor and went to park the tractor.

Dawn on the water. (*DM*)

Rowing down to the bank was a breeze. I had the tide with me, of course, and there was no wind. Oystercatchers were piping their delight as the ebb tide uncovered steadily more of their feeding grounds. At this time of year, especially in a good breeding season, it is not uncommon to see small parties of them flying up and down the shore. The familiar herd of mute swans was out between the Blimp and the Tangle. This is something I have not seen for many years, but we used to get gatherings of several dozen in August, all mature birds. Were these young adults who had not yet bred? Or non-breeders for some other reason? In any case, there were never any cygnets with them. One evening, rowing back late from the bank, the setting sun caught them, and a fleet of golden birds sailed past us. A curious sight at Kiltearn one year was an odd swan couple, a mute cob paired up with a whooper pen. Presumably, the whooper was a bird which couldn't fly and had therefore been left behind when her fellows flew north in the spring. I never discovered whether they attempted to breed.

By the time I reached the bank the sun was up, somewhat to the south of Invergordon as I saw it, as opposed to over the chimneys of the aluminium smelter, where it rises at midsummer. It was getting on for 6.00 am, two hours plus to low water. Perfect.

I set a killing stick through the ring in the head of the ground screw and twisted it well down into the sand. Then I pulled all the hint rope off the back of the boat so the beginning of the net was trailing in the shallows, and tied the rope to the screw. Now I was ready for action, and I pulled a few strokes out and stood up in the bow. While I waited, a single tern winged towards me along the shoreline. Nothing surprising about that – the bank holds a healthy population of sand eels, and the local common and Arctic terns often fish there. But this was a much smaller bird, a solitary little tern which must have crossed two firths from the nearest colony on the Moray shore.

One of the blessings of the bank is that there is deep water near the edge, so fish generally swim pretty close to it. In fact, wide shots are unlikely to succeed anyway – if the tide is running strongly, the net will be swept to one side, and if you get too far out, the water will be deeper than the net, the float rope is pulled under and fish escape over it. This was always an issue off the Cage at Alness, the cairn set right in the mouth of the river. There the channel was so close that you could only afford to go about 25 yards out before the net would sink. It could be frustrating watching the big heads go past – some of these were truly enormous, great heaves that you could easily see travelling downwind, perhaps a hundred grilse together, with multiple jumping, excited by the taste of their river – and know there was nothing you could do about them.

But a nice close shot was just what I wanted on the bank this morning, and sure enough, a tidy little shake appeared close in, well down the bank towards the lacers. He came on beautifully, giving me plenty time to lift the anchor and row a smooth shot round him, just wide enough to get the bag off. I was pretty sure I had him, so I took my time, pulling first the hint end of the net in until I had the bag centred, then taking in alternate wings and finally grasping all four ropes and dragging the bag up on to the sand. Three nice little grilsies. Piling the net was tedious, as I had to keep hopping across the backboard from ground rope to float rope, but the bank is so clean that there was scarcely any weed or any crabs in the net, so there was little need to stop and clean it as I piled.

A little later, I had a second shot, just a single fish this time, but a good one, somewhere about the 9lb mark. By this time the sun was high and the day was warm. I had long since got down to my T-shirt, and now it was time to go one better. I rowed out about 15 yards, threw out the anchor, stripped off and dived in. The water

A nine-pounder in the boat.

of the firth never becomes exactly warm, but this was heaven. The only warm-water swimming available locally is in the lagoon at the back of Balconie Point, when a big tide on a fine day floods the sun-kissed sea turf to a depth of a few feet. The same effect can sometimes be experienced on Kiltearn beach. We swam at the bank quite often, and on one memorable morning the Balconie Babes, having just been skinny-dipping, rowed a completely naked shot.

No more fish appeared this morning, but I had what I wanted – a good fish for the smoker, one for the family and two to sell to defray bothy expenses. What's more, when I got back to the bothy I had a keen appetite for bacon, eggs and tattie scones, and bragging rights over the crew when they finally appeared.

*   *   *

My second solo shot was on Balconie beach. Once again, this was at the tail end of a season, a good one and one of the last that we fished there. It was an evening high water, the regular crew had gone home, and I was waiting for some part-timers who had promised to come down. They didn't show. However, it was a very fishy-looking tide – a light but steady south-easterly breeze, rather dull overhead, but warm – so I decided to stick around.

Dave M watches the water, the old strainer in front of him. (*DM*)

Just outside the bothy door stood the remains of a larch strainer set in the ground, about two feet high. It must have been there a long time – it was split into three and worn to perhaps half its original circumference – but its core was still strong. It was rather in the way, and we had all stumbled over it at one time or another when the cry of 'Fish!' brought the crew running for the boat. But now it served what was probably its original purpose, to anchor one end of a net, and I tied the hint rope to it, sat on the east-wind bench and started watching the water.

For a long time, nothing much happened. The bothy gull patrolled the beach, occasionally dropping down on a scrap of food, probably the remains of our lunch. There was always a bothy gull, just a single common gull who made it his business to scavenge our leavings. A scattered colony of them nested around the edge of the old airfield, across the ford. As the tide crept in,

On the bothy bench. (*DM*)

a couple of skokers nosed along the edge of the beach below me, but I ignored them. They were obviously single fish, and although it was late in the season, I knew that there were better heads still around.

The water looked perfect. A steady ripple, easy on the eye, with big streaks of fresh hugging the shore then streaming out past Kiltearn towards the channel, giving himself the perfect lead-in. It was now getting on for high water. A couple of jumps in the distance failed to materialize into anything, and Henry appeared, cruising past the bothy about 100 yards out. Perhaps he was having better luck than I?

Then all of a sudden, as if out of nowhere as often happens, fish struck up just 50 yards away, close in to the shore. Perhaps he had swum in out of the deep and turned when he hit the shallows. But he had turned my way and looked promising, too – there was the unmistakeable wallow made by a good head.

All went well. He held his line along the shore and it was a nice close shot. I took each wing of the net in turn, then all four ropes together, and as the bag approached I could see that it was going to be a little shottie. Sure enough, when I dragged the bag up on to dry land, not without some effort, there were thirteen fish in it, ten grilse and three thumping salmon. I think I may have let out a yell of triumph, even though there was no one to hear me.

Once I had the net piled, the fish boxed and the boat at anchor, I sat back on the bench and poured myself a big dram. It occurred to me that the last half hour probably represented the summit of my fishing life, and perhaps I should quit while still ahead. I didn't, of course, but this was very nearly the end of the Balconie years, and a rather different sort of fishing lay ahead.

6

A Flash of Wings …

George Huntley (1946–2019)

George, an almost completely unpublished poet of great skill and sensitivity,
was a frequent visitor from the south to Balconie and Kiltearn.

A flash of wings
a whistle of alarm
& there they go
two oystercatchers
jinking down the shore;
down by Kiltearn
a stranger half at home
i watch them
joy returning to my eye

how long ago it all seems now
but the wind's the same
that cool midsummer wind
blowing across the water;
& those little waves
as ever
gently pulse & slap
against
the muddy stones & seaweed

a tranquil place, a carefree time,
seapinks & driftwood, laughter, rain,
& there outside the bothy
on its slatted bench
who but ourselves as we used to be
before the poison chilled us:
a random crew, all come to share
the glory of the fishing,
a congregation gathered

A 'random crew'. (L to R) Dave J, Rik, Steve & Robbie Sutcliffe, Tommy, Paul Major. (*RR*)

The net comes in. (*RR*)

on that short grey turf
whiling away
long hours of the summer
with smoke & chat
& furious brown tea
in clinking mugs
what held us there, in such suspense?
What were we waiting for?
That cry of *fish*
the sudden shout
when they're first sighted
close inshore,
that moment when we all
leap into action:
listen – those seaboots
hurtling down the shingle
& those scrambling oars
as the boat rows out to meet them,
circles back;
down by the water's edge
we stand & watch
as the net pours out unfurling at each stroke,
& brace ourselves
in twenty seconds' time
to seize a rope-end, haul fulfilment in ...

7

At Balconie

Of all the fishing stations, Balconie holds the chief place in my heart. It was where I first went to the fishing, and it saw our best days, between the mid-1970s and the late 1980s. When I came back to the fishing, after seven years away, it was my great good fortune that Balconie ('the strong place') was available. The Estate had decided to start working their half share of the Alness station, and Buller had moved there; this suited him pretty well – he was now in his sixties, Alness was closer to home and he only fished it every other day.

I started looking around for crew, and there was immediately one obvious candidate. I had first met Dave Jenkins years earlier in Israel, and although we had lost touch, there he was again in Ross-shire, accompanied now by a fiery, red-haired Finnish girl (Kim) who drove a big old Mercedes. Dave and I got on well – crucial, given the amount

Dave J at the bothy. (*Katja Jenkins*)

of time you spend with your fellow fishers – and we had plenty in common. Funnily enough, Buller had been at school with Dave's mum – 'Och aye, Gracie Grant, I mind her well.' After I had signed Dave up, Stan Armstrong, the Estate's head forester, told me never to mention his name to the laird. This was because Dave was under suspicion (fully justified, I'm sure) of poaching on the Estate. The culmination of this had come when the laird caught Dave fishing on the river where he shouldn't have been, and the following exchange ensued:

Laird: 'Hey, you!'
Dave (looking around innocently): 'Who, me?'
Laird: 'Who the hell do you think you are, fishing on my river?'
Dave (knowing full well who it was): 'I'm David Jenkins, and who the hell are you?'

This was typical of Dave; he never took kindly to authority or people throwing their weight around. But he had all the qualities a fisherman needs – patience, guile, decisiveness, strength, sense of humour and a great fund of stories. He also initiated the bothy parties which became a feature of the season. Sly, teasing, kind and capable, all animals and children loved Dave. You could add 'most women' to that too – he had a very special brand of mischievous charm. Sadly, he is no longer with us, but a few years ago, when he was already ill with the cancer which killed him, we had our last day's fishing together. Just the two of us, me in the boat and him on the cairn, old men now and less able to pull in that heavy net, but we had three shots and caught six fish. It was the best day of the season in every way.

In London during the winter after my first season skippering Balconie, I answered an advertisement in the *Evening Standard* for 'experienced gardeners' (which I wasn't), landed the job and found myself the sidekick and chauffeur of Eamonn Noel Scott,

Eddie fish. (*FC*)

known to all as Eddie (it used to be 'Eddie fish', nowadays it's 'Eddie spoons', which he plays) a red-haired and red-bearded fellow from Limerick. As I drove him around town maintaining gardens and window-boxes, and learning from him a lot about gardening, we became firm friends. He was getting restive in London, I knew I needed a first mate for the next season since Dave was moving on to open up the station at Foulis, and so I invited Eddie to try his hand on the firth.

At about the same time, Ben, a friend from school and university, appeared back in the UK from the Far East, where he had been working for one of the 'hongs', the

The crew between tides, Ben in the foreground.

great trading companies of Hong Kong, and then as a journalist covering the last stages of the Vietnam War. He was now training to be a doctor and fancied a summer vacation in the Highlands, so I invited him to join the party. Ben lived in the bothy, and this was occasionally a source of friction, because it was his 'home' while also serving as the kitchen and shelter of two hairy fishermen. Luckily, it was a fabulous summer, so we spent a lot of time outside. Ben swam in the firth every day, and when we asked him, as a budding medic, what to do for any cut, sprain, ache or ailment, his answer was always the same – 'Put it in the sea.' His determination to get to the heart of things, or people, gave us another lasting expression for this sort of digging deep – 'getting the scalpel out'.

Ben later forsook medicine and took up the philosophy of Rudolf Steiner, which he still follows. So for the next season Eddie and I had to find a third man. I can't remember how we fell in with James Stephen Webster, a lad from Wick known to all as Stevie Web, but he certainly filled the bill. He was at that time a neighbour of mine in Ardross, he was at a loose end and he had fishing experience, mostly on bag net stations on the north coast.

You couldn't have asked for a better crew than Eddie and Stevie, and these were our salad days: there were plenty of fish, prices were good and we lived the fishing to the full. For me the season began in April with painting of boats and repair of nets. By the end of the month the big coble would be in the water on the Alness station, and Buller and I would fish the month of May there together. Fish were never plentiful, but the weather, as often in the Highlands in May, was generally good, the spring fish run bigger than the summer grilse and prices were high.

Stevie Web.

The skipper, at Balconie. (DM)

In June I would move to Balconie and fish the month with Eddie. This meant, first, setting up the bothy. Built in a day by Buller and Mr Cheyne, the Estate carpenter, the bothy (the Tweed netsmen call theirs 'shiels') was a wooden cabin some ten feet by twelve, perched just above the high water mark on the very tip of Balconie Point. Here we lived, cooked our meals and fished the beach when the tide was in. The bothy had a tarred roof, a big shuttered window looking out to sea and a woodstove in the corner. Scaffold-board benches were fixed to the front, west and east walls, there was a lean-to at the back and a small secondary shed at the rear corner to the east – known, even when my girls had ceased to inhabit it, as 'the goat shed'. In the off-season the bothy was used by all sorts of people – sheltering wildfowlers, partying teenagers, perhaps even lovers with nowhere else to go – and we soon learned that there was no point trying to lock it; the inevitable break-ins only caused more damage than was already inflicted by casual vandalism.

Yet somehow we always managed to patch up the winter's scars and make it ready for the season. The bothy's 'furniture' consisted of the woodstove, a plain wooden store cupboard and the two-ring gas burner and grill which sat on top of it, some scraps of carpet, a few boxes of pots, pans, plates and cutlery, two 5-gallon plastic water containers (we brought all our water on the back of the tractor from the Black Rock

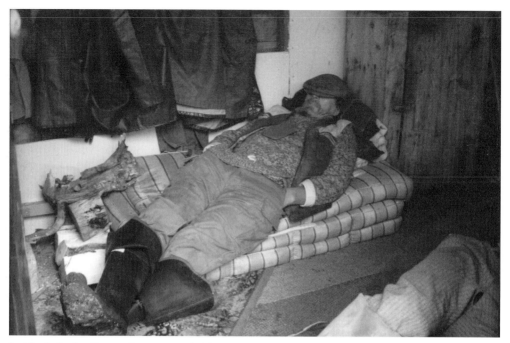

Inside the bothy. Doug taking it easy. (*FC*)

river), some mattresses, sheepskins and the occasional ornament (notably a life-size rubber lobster which hung from the ceiling). This was all stored in a former RAF hangar, where the boats spent the winter, on the site of the present Estate sawmill. We were even quite house-proud about our temporary home. At the beginning of one season my diary records, 'Tidied the bothy. New carpet!', and at the end of every fishing week we would shake out the soft furnishings, sweep the floor and throw shovelfuls of fresh gravel from the beach around the door and the outside benches. Non-burnable rubbish went into a 40-gallon oil drum behind the bothy, and at the end of the season we would bury it. I sometimes wondered what some future archaeologist, investigating the lives of salmon fishers, would make of our leavings.

June could be fairly quiet on the fishing front. In Eddie's first ever fortnight at Balconie I think he saw only one fish caught, and that was a chancy shot at a jumper. He must have wondered what he had let himself in for. But it was just a slow start, and we ended the season with close to a thousand fish. June's weather is often worse than May's – I have actually seen snow falling at the bothy early in the month – but there were compensations. This was the tail-end of the Highland spring, the rabbit-cropped turf of the Point would be sprinkled with wild flowers – daisies, campion, lady's bedstraw, vetch and bird's-foot trefoil – the whins were still out and the birds were singing. I have rarely felt more at peace than when lying flat on my back on the grass there between tides, listening to glorious lark music in a blue sky above. I found the lark's nest to the east of the bothy, four delicious little brown eggs half covered by a dome of rough grass.

Once the Point had a fine stand of Scots pines, but today just one remains. The rest were blown down in a great gale in the 1950s, and some of their trunks were still lying around, handy fuel for the bothy stove. Their place was taken by a group of Corsican pines (*Pinus nigra*) planted by Stan behind the bothy, tough characters which spread to form a mighty thicket. Every June, there would come one fine day when the pines gave off huge clouds of pollen. If you pushed through them with your spade, looking for a quiet spot to do your business, you would emerge covered in yellow dust.

The trees also sheltered a caravan, where Eddie, sometimes accompanied by his Australian girlfriend Chris, stayed during the season. I occasionally used the caravan for a kip between tides, and it was there in July 1981, after a morning's fishing that had not gone well, that I drifted off to sleep listening to Test Match Special, my mood not improved by England collapsing to 135 for 7 and being about to lose to Australia. I slept for a couple of hours, thereby missing all Botham's Headingley heroics.

The fishermen's ladies – Jan, Barbara, Brenda and Chris – spent a fair bit of time at the bothy, and our other regular companions were Freddie the dachshund and Suzie and Luschka, white Saanen goats, who provided our milk, cropped the grass and browsed the bushes along the track to the ford. Freddie often came out to low water with us and slept in the bow of the boat on a sheepskin or in a big padded sack. She did not like to be parted from her master; the first time I tried to leave her on the cairn, she immediately jumped in the water and swam out to join me in the boat. All three animals were extremely greedy – woe betide you if you ran down the beach for a shot and left any food unattended. The goats would have your tobacco, too.

The skipper asleep. (*DM*)

The girls looking out of their shed. (*ES*)

The old bothy.

A hundred yards or so to the west of the bothy – or, I should say, where the bothy once stood, for no trace of it now remains – there is a ruin at the edge of the water. The Highland Historic Environment Record describes this as a 'building designed to look like a chapel with arched windows etc. but is actually a fishing station. C.7m by 5m. Gable walls complete but side walls tumbled.' When I first knew Balconie, the old bothy still had part of its roof, and Buller remembered it being used, at least for storage. Oddly, however, it is some way from the actual Point and therefore not perfectly sited to fish from. Buller picked absolutely the right spot when he planned the new bothy.

We sometimes speculated that the arched window suggested a connection with Castlecraig,

Castlecraig. (*DM*)

directly opposite on the Black Isle shore. This sixteenth-century tower, four storeys high but ruinous, is believed to have been built on the site of the summer palace of the pre-Reformation Bishops of Moray and Ross, and we liked to imagine the bishop being rowed across to hold services in our tiny chapel.

* * *

The weeks that made or broke your season were those of the grilse run. Nowadays it is less predictable, and the grilse do not arrive in numbers. In fact, it may be that we are seeing a change in a natural cycle towards more spring or autumn fish and many fewer grilse. But in those days Buller's dictum held true: 'When the year turns, look for your first grilse.' One such day sticks in the memory, in the first season I was back at Balconie. It was late June, a pal from London had come to stay and I was keen to show him some action, but we had only had the odd fish so far. Low water was around midday, a smallish tide, and the weather was perfect for the Skiach – dull and slightly misty, a good breeze from the west. The water had a really 'fishy' look, and sure enough, a nice-looking head soon struck up. I was on my own in the boat and, still new to skippering and over-excited at the sight of fish, I shouted to the crew, sat down to the oars and started to row. But something was wrong; I didn't seem to be making any progress. I had forgotten to lift the anchor! Somehow, despite the resulting scramble and the noise of a hurriedly yanked anchor banging against the side of the boat, I managed to get round the head. Eight grilsies, fat, shiny and fresh from the sea, and before the tide was done we had had five more. The season had started.

At the end of June, Stevie would join Eddie and me, and the Balconie Babes were complete, ready to tackle the grilse run and see the season out to its legal end on 26 August and the bothy party

Stevie Web. (*DM*)

which celebrated it. Stevie died not long ago, one of many fishers who have left us before their time. At his funeral, the celebrant read out some of what I had written about him:

> At the fishing Stevie very quickly learned all the tricks of the trade. If he was there, you just knew you would get fish – Eddie said to me just the other day, 'Stevie was a reverse Jonah!' He never complained about four o'clock starts, long days or bad weather. He made the best coffee, in a beat-up old percolator. He rolled the finest joints. He was always good for a laugh, or for a long meditative conversation when you were waiting for fish. One season, with Dave 'Woolly-Hat' McLachlan, he even fished with a leg in plaster – that's how good a fisherman he was.
>
> Stevie was always super-tidy and stylish, in his person and in his belongings. I can see him now, in neatly pressed jeans and that jaunty skipper's cap which he found on the tideline and refurbished. It suited him perfectly.
>
> At work – he was an electrician by trade – Stevie was as neat and competent as he was at everything else. Unlike some tradesmen, who suck their teeth and tell you a thing you want is impossible, Stevie would always come up with an answer. He was a solutions man, never a problems one.

We were convinced that Balconie was the finest fishing station in Scotland, and looking back I see no reason to doubt it. You could fish low water and high in east or west wind, fresh water pulls fish in towards rivers at each end of the station, and, best of all, there was Balconie Point itself. The Point, a spit of rough grass, the Corsican pines and salt marsh, difficult to get at except by fording the Black Rock River or tramping along the

Stevie backs the boat in at high water. (*RR*)

shore, was our little kingdom and the bothy was our castle. On fine days the bothy was a magnet for friends who had nothing particular to do in those happy times; but almost best of all were the long days when we had the place to ourselves, and the big event was the arrival of Stan's Land Rover bucking down the track to come and collect the fish.

Stan the forester was our liaison man with the Estate. You couldn't have had a better one – he loved the fishing and would usually hang on for a cup of tea and the chance of a shot. He had an expert eye for fish and, like Stevie Web, he was a 'reverse Jonah' – when he was there, things nearly always went well. When we took an occasional day off, for the Black Isle Show or the St Boniface Fair in Fortrose, Stan would bring his own crew down and fish Balconie. He took care of the tedious business of getting fish to market: driving them into Dingwall for the Aberdeen or Glasgow train, dealing with complaints from the merchants ('Your fish were soft when they arrived') and later on, driving them to Bannerman's in Tain. He knew how to turn a blind eye when appropriate; 'p.s.' in my diary is code for 'private sale', and all the housekeeping, food and drink for the bothy we covered by selling fish on the side, as Stan well knew, but

Social life at the bothy. (L to R) Eddie, Stevie Web, Barbara, Doug. Note the cans of McEwans Export. (*FC*)

he said nothing. It was hard to persuade him to take a fish himself, however. A big, broad, red-faced fellow, he was the kindest and most generous of men. On the quiet, he did many a good deed to help folk in need, and I shall never forget the haunch of venison he once gave us; it came from a 'yeld' (barren) hind, an animal that had never undergone the rigours of the rut and calving, and the delicious gamey meat simply fell off the bone when we barbecued it at a bothy party. We tried to pick a night at the end of the season with a fullish moon and a night-time high water to hold the party. The early do's were quite modest affairs – a few friends of the fishing and other pals and neighbours – but they soon grew, and the later ones attracted not a few gate-crashers. The recipe was simple: collect

Discussing tactics with Stan in his Land Rover. (*ES*)

Eddie and Stevie inspect the barbecue pit before a bothy party. (*ES*)

Party time at the bothy. (L to R) Steve K, Gerald, Chris, Fionna, self. (*FC*)

plenty driftwood and dig a pit in the beach in front of the bothy – this served as a barbecue and, when the food was all gone, for illumination and warmth; Highland nights can be quite nippy by the end of August. Lay in some meat and fish for the barbecue and a moderate foundation of drink – guests were expected to (and did) bring salads, desserts and alcohol of their own. Music was occasionally live, but more often supplied by a car stereo. The evenings would start decorously enough but became pretty wild by the end. At some point the boat would be launched, and trips on the water were offered. It was not unknown to row across to the Black Isle. I recall leaving one party in the early hours, somewhat the worse for wear and with the boat still in the water, and mumbling to Eddie, 'See you look after the boat.' That was the night that he and Wanda got stranded on a musselbank. Happy days.

In general, we fed very well at the bothy. There were plenty of fry-ups and shop-bought cakes, of course, but insofar as two gas rings and a grill allowed, we also made more ambitious meals. Soups and stews were popular, and here are a couple that we enjoyed:

Dougie's Cullen Skink

500g smoked haddock
Good knob of butter
1 onion, peeled and chopped
1 leek, cut into pieces
2 medium potatoes, peeled and cut into chunks
500ml whole milk
Small pot of double cream

1. Put the fish into a pan with half the milk and the same amount of water and simmer for 10 minutes.
2. In another pan sweat the onion and the leek until soft, and season with black pepper.
3. Add the potato chunks, pour in the haddock cooking liquor and simmer until the potato is tender.
4. Meanwhile, remove skin and any bones from the haddock, and break it up into flakes.
5. Add the rest of the milk, the cream and the haddock to the pan, mash roughly with a fork, heat up and serve.

This soup is just the ticket on a cold day, when there's a gale outside, the boat is out of the water, the stove is lit and everyone is huddled in the bothy.

One of the pleasures of bothy cooking is having to be creative with the ingredients that happen to be at hand. Popping to the shop wasn't easy, and it was always something of a culture shock leaving the world of Balconie Point and entering the village Spar. One day, Eddie and I, clutching Eddie's typically tiny shopping list inscribed on the flap of a Rizla packet, a bit dazed after an early morning tide and probably a bit stoned as well, bumped into the young laird's new wife in the village. We just about managed to exchange pleasantries, and later I heard that she had said, after meeting these two long-haired and bearded figures, with their thigh boots and earrings, 'I was in the village this morning and I think I just met the Estate pirates.'

Another favourite dish was 'snag stew'. All sorts of things can go into it, especially other veg, depending on what's in the cupboard, but the basics are something like this:

'The Estate pirates' taking time off at a wedding. (*ES*)

Snag Stew

1lb of butcher's sausages ('snags'), cut into 2in pieces
4 rashers of bacon chopped small
2 medium onions, chopped
Garlic (we used wild garlic leaves from the riverbank)
1 small tin of tomatoes
Several good handfuls of green or brown lentils
Seasoning, including a good dash of Lea & Perrins
Beer

1. Cover the lentils with beer and simmer slowly.
2. In another pan, sweat the onion in butter or oil, then remove and add to the lentil pan.
3. Fry the sausage pieces and the chopped bacon.
4. Once the lentils are soft, drain off the liquid and keep it.
5. Add the sausages, bacon, tomatoes and seasoning to the lentils, stir well and add the liquid to achieve the consistency you prefer. More beer can be added if necessary.
6. Stir the garlic leaves in at the last moment, and serve with tatties or hunks of bread for mopping.

Oz (left), one of the kindest and funniest of men, with Angus, an occasional fisherman. (*Lucy Moseley*)

We generally had plenty of beer; this was down to my father, who visited regularly and never failed to take a few cans with him.

On fine days we often had visitors, provided that they knew how to get to the bothy – this meant either a trek through the fields and along the shore, or wading across the ford. When the water was low, the ford was driveable in a vehicle with reasonable clearance. My Renault 4 crossed it a good few times. But not everyone succeeded. Oz, a regular visitor and fisherman, arrived on foot one day at the bothy. We assumed he had parked on the other side of the ford and walked across, and he sat down, accepted a cup of coffee, shared his cunning wee pipe with us and chewed the fat for an hour or so. Then it suddenly occurred to me that he had his parents staying with him.

'What are your folks doing today, Oz?'

'They're with me.'

I looked around. 'Where are they?'

'Oh, they're in the ford.'

Quite happy to be relieved of their company for a while, Oz had driven his poor old mum and dad into the river, deliberately (I think) grounded the car and left them there, saying he would go and get help and giving them strict instructions to stay put, because the current was dangerous. We eventually pulled them out with the tractor.

Probably our most frequent visitor was Davy, a pub landlord and one of Buller's regulars. He always took something with him from his garden – my fondest memory is of his early tatties, Sharpe's Express or Duke of York, with that slightly crumbly texture and earthy flavour that only a freshly-dug new potato possesses. Although I had known Davy for many years, he was slightly suspicious of some of our ways – offered a cup of Lapsang Souchong, he refused it nervously, and we later discovered

The biggest fish of the season (21lbs). (L to R) Ben, self, Eddie, Davy.

that he thought it was 'drugs'. He was a very useful hand, however, and always ready with a quip. If things were going badly, or fish were scarce, he would say to me, 'Ah, George boy, it'll be Arthurville for you this winter!' This was the local old folk's home and former poor house.

Wilf the gamekeeper was another visitor. He was a gnome-like figure, a stalker, a slinker and (some said) a bit of a voyeur, and he would always appear without warning from the trees at the back of the bothy. You never saw him coming. A Norfolk man transplanted to the Highlands long ago, he had never lost his East Anglian twang, and he had the hard, slightly sinister air of a man whose business was killing things. I used to go shooting pigeons with him, and he was a dead shot. Waiting in the edge of a wood for pigeons to come in to roost one winter afternoon, Wilf spotted a couple of hoodie crows flying across us in the distance. In a flash he had his hand cupped to his mouth and gave out a perfect imitation of the hoodie's slightly strangled caw. Sure enough, the birds changed direction and flew towards us. He shot them both.

With Wilf (centre) and Bobby, another gamekeeper and a regular fisherman. (*ES*)

Another old stager who visited us often was Sonny, from the village. A delightful fellow, and a good gardener, but we had a feeling that he might be a bit of a Jonah. This business of Jonahs was something that Buller firmly believed in, and I do think there is something in it. If a Jonah is present, something will often go wrong – fish swim outside the boat or cut in suddenly under the rope; the net sticks or rolls round the ground rope; worst of all are the times when everything seems to have gone right but the net comes in empty. There are several sorts of Jonah: clumsy people are obvious targets, as are the noisy, over-keen and expectant; in contrast, gloom merchants are just as bad. But sometimes it's nothing you can put your finger on – you just know that if so-and-so is there you had better watch out. One July day, my diary has 'Jonah'd out of a good head by Ian'. I cannot remember who the unfortunate Ian was, but he was clearly one of them.

Fishermen are notoriously superstitious creatures. If an old fisherman passed a minister or a woman with ginger hair on the way to his boat he might well refuse to go to sea that day. It was strictly forbidden to say the words 'pig' or 'rabbit' on a boat – if you really had to mention the animals you called them 'curly tail' or 'bob tail' instead. A particular prohibition, and one that we keep up as best we can, is on the word 'salmon', something few fishermen care to say aloud, whatever they are fishing for. Some call them 'the reid fish', but we adopted a Caithness usage from Stevie Web: if you hear the s-word or use it accidentally, you can clear the bad luck it brings by declaring, 'Cold

Steve Sutcliffe (left) watching the water with Hector Munro and Eddie.

iron'. We just call them 'fish'. Sea trout, mullet, flounders, we are happy to name, but if we say plain 'fish' then it is himself that we mean.

Another curse which I saw strike a good many times was what happens if you go for the killing sticks (some fishermen call them 'priests' or 'nabbies', other talk of 'felling sticks') before the shot is in. This was an absolute law of Buller's, and one of the very few occasions that I saw him angry was when I broke it as a novice. I had seen a few shots by then, there were plenty hands on the ropes and I was standing around spare as the net came in. Wanting to be helpful and part of the action, I reached into the bow to pick up the sticks. Luckily, Buller saw what I was at before I actually had one in my hand. 'Drop that!' he said sharply, and later read me a lecture about what would have happened if I had touched them. I never did it again, but it taught me in future to keep an eye on over-enthusiastic boys. Of course, I didn't always manage to, and on a number of occasions they caused us to lose fish.

There are good omens, too. A bumblebee flying over the boat is a sign of fish to come; and a fish which has already been knocked on the head but flaps his tail under the backboard is calling to his mates to come along and get caught too.

Not many strangers made their way to the bothy, but Tommy and Steve, a couple of lads from the village in their early teens, began to show up pretty regularly. At first they kept their distance and nervously refused our offers of a seat or a cup of tea. But gradually they came in closer as they got accustomed to us, and eventually they accepted food and drink. It was a bit like taming wild animals. Then they began to take a hand on a rope when we had a shot, and by the end of that season they were coming out to low water with us. Steve in particular developed a really good eye for fish. In the later Kiltearn years, now middle-aged and with a family, he often came down for an evening tide, and if the fishing had carried on I had him in mind as the man to take it over – he was local, he could spot fish and he was approaching the age when he might have some time on his hands. But it was not to be.

8

Netting the Scottish Fish

Andrew McNeillie

Not so many miles north of Cawdor
nor in the worst of tide or weather
the netsmen aboard their coble
and their fellows on the cairn,
study every fold and quibble
of light on the water through July...
Never naming what they look to see,
they call a fish a fish, from superstition.
And today again the unnameable
remains ineffable, invisible
to all but the inward eye. A condition
with a long history here.

Andrew, fisherman, poet and publisher, spent a week on the water with us a few years ago. We didn't get many fish ('the unnameable remains ineffable'), but Andrew himself spent many hours casting a lure for sea trout and was rewarded with a nice two-pounder – one of the very few I have ever seen taken on a rod in the firth; Rik and Dave regularly trolled a spinner from Balachladdich beach to Kiltearn and back and never caught a one. Andrew was also very taken with our superstitious unwillingness to name the fish we were after, and he invited me to write a piece under the title 'Cold Iron' (the old fishers' term to clear any bad luck provoked by saying 'salmon') for Archipelago, *his then newly founded magazine of nature writing (www.clutag-archipelago.com).*

The poem is included by kind permission of Carcanet Press, publishers of Andrew's collection of verse, In Mortal Memory.

9

Fisher Men

Not everyone is cut out for the fishing. The eager and impatient do not find it to their taste; in fact, they are more than likely to spoil the tide with misplaced expectation. There is no answer to questions like 'Do you think we are going to catch fish today?' You can say conditions are good, the wind is a moderate, steady breeze from west or east, it's not too bright, there were fish about yesterday, there's a good crew out today. But none of this guarantees fish. Maybe it will be a day when things go wrong – the net sticks then comes off in a lump, fish cut out at the last

Still fishing after all these years. (L to R) Jura, self, Steve K, Eddie, Oz, Stevie Web. (*RR*)

Regulars and occasionals. (L to R) Rod, self, Jonathan, Dave J, Youssuf, Jura. (*JH*)

A bunch of old fishers. (L to R) Dave J, Oz, Steve K, self, Rik. (*JH*)

minute, fish cut in at the last minute and swim under the rope, fish slip under the ground rope as the net comes ashore. Maybe the fish are there but all we see are jumps in the channel or heads cruising tantalizingly out of reach. Or maybe we see nothing at all except the water and the birds and the sky. That's fishing for you.

Four or five hours standing out in a boat or on a little cairn are a fair test, and those who don't take to it rarely come back for a second tide. But fortunately there has always been a hard core who love it, who are prepared to be there at first light for an early tide, who cheerfully sit out a wet day and who know how important it is to seize the chance when fish do come.

As on a war memorial, I record below the names of those I fished with regularly over the years and who are no longer with us:

Stan Armstrong
Buller Black
Davy Bremner
Doug Chalmers
Wanda Jamrozik
David Jenkins
Gary McCrossan
Oz Moseley
Paul Przypisny
Kenny Robertson
Stevie Webster

It would be impossible to record everyone who has spent time at the fishing. At the end of one fairly recent season, I totted up thirty names – regulars, occasionals, friends, relations, visitors, drop-ins. There must have been hundreds over the years. A rough count of people who have been frequent fishers came to around forty.

The craic has always been half the fun of the fishing. The way we fish leaves plenty of time (sometimes too much) between shots; time to chat, to have a smoke, a cup of tea, a biscuit, a dram. The hours of water-watching are also hours of talk, and there is something about standing watching the water together which invites confidences. You get to know your fellow fishers pretty well.

10

A Million Hands Clapping

It is one of the last Balconie seasons, and the fishers have begun to disperse. Eddie has got himself a job at Ardross Castle, Stevie Web is working as a sparkie. I am living away, doing a second degree at Lancaster University, but back for the summer and staying with my mother. My regular crew is Dick, a near neighbour I can easily collect in the mornings. Today he has brought his son with him, a little boy of about seven.

It's a fine morning with a light westerly breeze, and we are fishing high water at the bothy. As far as I can recall, it is just Dick and I, no third crewman. The boy is happily playing along the beach, collecting stones and shells and turning over mats of seaweed on the high water mark to look for sandhoppers. It's warm, and occasionally he comes back to the bothy for a sip of Coke. Dick and I are sitting on the front bench – there's no need for shelter today, and we might get a sight of fish coming either way. Dick has not been at the game long, but he is beginning to develop an eye for them.

There hasn't been a lot doing yet, but there are fish around, and we have seen some good heads in the last few days. We see a couple of jumps, way off, out from the mouth of the Black Rock. As so often, nothing comes of these, at least to begin with, but then I can see something swimming, as far out as the jumps but a little closer to us. To begin with, I doubt if it's fish. The sight on the water is good – a nice steady ripple – but it's a long way away to be able to see himself. Probably it's Henry, I think, swimming high. He often deceives us. Especially in the calm, you see something making a really good water a long way off and you start to get excited; then the big, shiny, black head pops up and your hopes die.

This time, though, it's not the seal. There are more jumps, and just when I have resigned myself to the fact that he is going to keep motoring along in the deep, well out of our reach, he suddenly turns in and starts heading straight for the shore. Now I begin to think we could be in for something special. The swim is very broad, as if there are several fish leading in parallel, and there is more jumping. As he comes in closer he looks even better – he's making a water on a really broad front, almost like a shoal of mackerel when it shimmers just under the surface.

Now I'm faced with a problem. He is heading straight in towards the beach, and when he hits it, what will he do? Turn round and head out again, of course, but which way? In any case, it is now time to move. I get in the boat and tell Dick to give me plenty rope. For some reason we are talking in whispers. The head is still coming in, and I row out gingerly about twenty yards, slightly upwind of his course and hang there, standing up and waiting, banking on the belief that when he does turn he will keep going west.

He's still coming, now almost as close in as the boat and swimming fast, and I have to make my mind up.

'Pull a bit off, Dick' – this in a whisper again.

Perhaps ten feet of net come off, and I sit down to the oars. Now the leading fish hit shallow water a few feet from the beach, and the water boils as they all turn and head out.

'Pull away!'

It's impossible to tell which way they are going to go, but I know that if I can get across them I stand a chance, so I row like crazy, a really wide shot, no more than twenty yards out but as far as I can downwind, before I turn back to the shore.

A boat full of fish. (*FC*)

'You're OK!' yells Dick, and indeed, I have seen the fish – or the bulk of them; some may well have doubled back and got out before I could get round them – swim towards the bag.

Back on shore, we take a couple of ropes each and start to take the net in. It's awkward, because of the shape of the shot I rowed, but we gradually move closer to each other, taking net in all the while, until we have it in a good loop. Meanwhile, there is plenty activity inside the net – jumps, birls against the floats and the tugging on the float rope which tells of a fish gilled.

As the bag comes close to the beach, the activity in the net becomes ever more frantic. I warn Dick to take a deep breath and give it his all, and with a yell we pull the bag up on to dry land. It's an immense spread of fish, and they go mad, flapping their tails on the stones. Killing them takes a good few minutes, and we stand up from the net with our faces covered in salt water, sand and scales.

Now, standing back, the sheer number of fish hits me. We fetch a couple of boxes each, then another couple, and count as we fill them. It's sixty-three fish, all smallish grilse apart from a few around the 10lb mark, and the biggest shot I have ever seen.

Dick's little boy has been watching all this, wide-eyed. When the net is piled, the boat is at anchor and we are finally back on the bench with a cup of tea and a roll-up, I hear him say to his father, 'Dad, you know when you pulled the net in and those fish were all on the beach, it sounded like a million hands clapping.'

11

Early Days

I was just a boy when I was first at the fishing. Sixteen, maybe seventeen. Young enough to be told what to do – push the boat out, box those fish, coil that rope – but old enough to pull the net against a big tide on the sandbank or take an oar against a strong west wind on the row back to the bothy.

Buller Black had the fishing at Balconie in these days. James was his given name, but 'Buller' fitted his rounded, broad shoulders and his full ruddy cheeks. He was not always the quickest of men on the uptake away from the water, but by God he knew the fishing – not just the practical matters of care for boat and net or the tactics of where to fish in any given combination of wind and tide, but the essence of it: his patience was inexhaustible, he could spot fish anywhere, and when they did appear he reacted

Buller goes fishing. (*Black family*)

Early days at the fishing. Self third left, the Brigadier (in braces) at far right.

with speed and decision. One evening at the height of the season we were fishing high water when a gale blew up. 'This is no good', he said, 'we'll away up to the pub.' The rest of the crew went home, but Mary his wife, who cooked for us and kept house in the bothy, stayed behind, and so did I. Just finishing our drinks – pints for Buller and me, vodka and lemonade for Mary – he looked out of the window. 'The wind's dropped. Come on, we'd best be back down there.' It was as if he could smell them. With Mary on the rope and the two of us in the boat, we rowed shot after shot and ended the tide with almost a hundred fish.

That was in the good old days, probably in 1967, the summer of love for some, although the closest I got to it was sitting on the bothy bench listening to 'San Francisco (Be Sure to Wear Flowers in Your Hair)' on my transistor. At Balconie this was the big year, over three thousand fish, big heads putting up a great wallow as they swam up the firth; fish in the muddy black shallows on the musselbanks, fish in the clean deep water off the sandbank, fish by the rocky cairns at the mouth of the Skiach, fish swimming close in to the pebbles of Balconie beach itself. Then fish caught – shots of twenty, thirty, forty were commonplace – and fish to be boxed. As the 'loon' – a boy or apprentice in north-east Scotland – this was my job. Twenty grilse to a coffin-shaped wooden box marked with the merchant's name, 'Scotsal' or 'Wotherspoon'. Two layers of ten packed on their backs in fives, tail to tail. In these days they all went off by train to Aberdeen and Glasgow, so we kept great blocks of ice covered in sawdust in the lean-to behind the bothy to keep them fresh on the journey. Chip some pieces off the block with a hatchet, swill them in the sea, then scatter them over the fish. Boxing the fish was always done in the firth so that box and fish were thoroughly cleaned and soaked in salt water. Fresh water makes the fish go soft, but the sea preserves them. And it is important to get your fish off quickly to market. As we used to say:

Too much time from sea to seller
Turns salmon into salmonella

It was a two-man job to carry the hundredweight or so of each box up the beach by its rope handles; or if there were many boxes, they could be balanced on the boat trailer and towed up the beach by the old grey Fergie tractor.

When I fished with Buller, it was a month's job in school holidays and university vacations, when an extra hand was needed at the height of the season. I suspect it was my father's idea, tired of seeing me hanging around the house with nothing to do. He ('the Brigadier') was the factor to the Estate, the owners of the fishing rights at Balconie. Factors once had a poor reputation in the Highlands; running estates for often absentee proprietors, a good many abused their powers. The most notorious was Patrick Sellar, factor to the Sutherland estates in the first half of the nineteenth century, who was responsible for some of the cruellest evictions of tenants in what became known as the Highland Clearances. The Brigadier was a very different sort of chap, however. Schooled in the paternalistic tradition that an officer's job is to look after the men under his command, he acted as a very necessary conduit between the shy and rather chilly laird and his tenants and workers. These were the days when the Estate employed all its own tradesmen and labourers: a mason, joiner, plumber, mechanic, and so on. A bunch of them used to turn up at weekends to cut the Brigadier's hedges, clear his gutters and drains and generally tidy the place up, and he always made sure they had plenty of beer.

Geordie, the Estate mechanic (catchphrase: 'Aye, that's what I'm saying'), was a particular pal. He serviced the grey Fergie tractors we used at the fishing, kept our cars on the road and found second-hand vehicles for us. Geordie was not a habitual drinker, but he was one of those who couldn't stop at just one; once he started he had to finish the bottle, and woe betide you if you refused his offer of a dram. Eddie and I had one or two almost fatal sessions in his company. Despite Geordie's expertise, one day the Balconie tractor failed to start and we towed the boat down to the Skiach with the Land Rover to fish low water. On the way back, with the tide coming in, I carelessly drove through a patch of quicksand and got stuck. Nothing we tried would move her, and there was no time to get help before the tide came in. I had the presence of mind to take the battery out, but then all we could do was watch as the water covered her. A photograph exists somewhere of the roof as it disappears beneath the waves. Geordie laughed like a drain when I confessed what had happened – I suspect he thought we were a feckless lot, not to be trusted with machinery (he wasn't wrong) – and once the Rover had been recovered, towed up to his workshop and thoroughly hosed down, he gave Eddie and me a big bucket of diesel and a couple of brushes and told us to wash her all over, inside and out. This we did, then Geordie took her into the garage and got to work.

Amazingly, he got her going again, and that Land Rover ran quite happily for several more years. She was 1950s vintage, old and very shabby; perhaps it should have been no surprise one evening, when a couple of girls hitch-hiking refused our offer of a lift, after two hairy fishermen beckoned to them out of the back. The Rover was also very heavy on petrol – except when Eddie once filled her with diesel by mistake, another occasion for Geordie to have some fun at our expense – but the ideal transport to negotiate the rough road to the bothy and fetch and carry fishing gear. When I finally came to sell her, the registration number, JSO 357, was worth more than the vehicle.

When I first fished with Buller, although I didn't realize it at the time, it must have been tricky for him having the factor's son in his crew. It wasn't that he was afraid of telling me what to do – although he was a mild man and not given to barking orders – more that there were certain things he didn't want the boss to know. Buller's deal (and mine, later) was as follows: during the season the Estate paid him a wage, then he got a share of the profits, and the regular crew got a bonus calculated on the catch. In 1967 Buller bought himself a fire-engine red Ford Corsair with his share. The fish, when caught, were technically the property of the laird, but not all of them ended up going off to the merchant. Unofficially, a certain number stayed with the fishers: the first fish of the season, by tradition, was never sold; the regular crew would take at least one fish home at the end of every week; other helpers, especially if there were plenty fish going, could expect to get one now and again – extra hands were always welcome, and this way, they would come back for more; then there were some 'friends of the fishing' who needed to be kept sweet – landowners whose ground we had to cross to get to the shore, for example. The first few times I saw Buller slip a fish to one of the crew he muttered some apologetic remark, but pretty soon he saw that I wasn't going

Learning the fishing at Balconie with Buller and Mary. (*Black family*)

to blab, and in any case I got to take the odd fish home myself. Sea trout we never sold or declared. However often a request came down for one for the laird's table, the same reply went back: 'Sorry, we never get any.'

I learned fast from Buller and was soon using the lingo naturally – heads, shots, making a water, and so on. I still come out sometimes with remarks that he used to make – if two consecutive shots contained a pair of fish, he would say, 'Aye, they're nesting.' A riper comment when we had a shot of two fish came from Paul the Pole: he would mime sliding one down his wader and announce, 'One for you, one for me – and fucka da lairdie!'

Learning to see fish was trickier, mostly because I didn't have the patience to concentrate on watching the water. But gradually I learned to distinguish the urgent signs of underwater life from jabble, current and the mark of sprats or a troutie's jump. I'm afraid that no one will ever learn this art again; even if the fishing had not come to an end, there simply aren't enough fish now for anyone to learn what they look like in all conditions of light and wind. When the present generation (none of us is much under sixty) pass on, the skill will be gone forever.

To begin with, I was always left on the rope, but then I graduated to the occasional session in the boat with Buller, and this is where I learned most. Sometimes he would put me to watching upwind for jumps, or to keep an eye one way in a calm, but mostly we looked the same way. Buller always saw fish before I did; he was somehow able to

Buller killing fish, while Mary looks on. (*Black family*)

watch the water a hundred yards away and more and at the same time stay alert to fish which might pop up closer to the boat. He passed on a good deal of fishing lore: about his grandfather, who had worked many stations and from whom he learned his skill; what to do if there was an oil spill (go home – these must have been quite frequent in the days when the Navy used Invergordon); where to fish in which conditions – no use going to the bank in an east wind, but the same wind is the only time to fish the Alness beach; tales of Foxy Fraser, his old rival, who would stop at nothing, even using an illegal gill net. Buller hardly ever broke the rules, though he occasionally bent them; on a really misty morning, when it was difficult to see the water and we were pretty much invisible ourselves, I have seen him sit out in the boat with a length of net run out in a hook and watch the float rope for the birl of a fish. This technique, known as 'toot and haul' (the man in the boat gives a toot when he sees fish, then the man on the bank hauls), is strictly speaking illegal – the law says your net must be moving at all times – but if you can't see fish, what are you going to do?

In later years, when I had my skipper's ticket and Buller and I would fish Alness together in May, I got to know him better. He and I would be in the boat, with Paul, or sometimes Buller's brother Pattie, on the rope. Early morning tides would start with Buller taking a big pinch of mentholated snuff and sneezing hugely ('clears the heid'). Although I recall one May tide on the Bell when we caught thirteen fish in thirteen shots – hard work, all big single fish, no blanks – there were rarely many fish at this time of year, so plenty of things were required to 'break the monotony' – coffee and a piece, a dram, a roll-up for me (Buller didn't smoke much, apart from the occasional cigar) and his favourite tipple, Tennent's lager, usually one of the 'lager lovelies' series, with Ann, June, Penny, Lorraine or some other soft-porn pin-up on the can. When he finished his cans Buller simply tossed them into the firth, but I said nothing. Having consumed a couple of cans, he would drop one knee expertly on to the gunwale and 'sweeten the water' or 'give himself a taste' – other sayings I found myself adopting in later years as my own bladder grew weaker with age. Occasionally there were tales of his military service in Palestine after the war – that tricky period when Britain was trying to hold the ring between Arabs and Jews – or football talk. Buller was a big Rangers fan and had been a considerable performer himself, playing on the wing for Ross County in his younger days.

At the bothy in those days there was a fine cast of characters. Mary Black, a hardy Orcadian, would be there most days, knitting, reading *My Weekly* and cooking our meals. She would take a hand on the rope at the beach if required, but never came out to low water with us. Fishermen have traditionally believed women to be bad luck in the boat, and there were some sideways looks when we first took them out, but there have been some excellent female fishers over the years: Gillian and Fiona Munro, Fionna Chalmers, Romay Garcia, the late Wanda Jamrozik, Ischa Warmerdam.

The most frequent visitor in Buller's day was Davy Bremner, landlord of the Station Hotel in Alness. Davy was no ordinary publican but a government employee. In a curious hangover of the First World War, nineteen pubs around the Cromarty Firth

Mary Black. (*Black family*)

A lady fisher. (*DM*)

were then still under state control, and remained so until 1973. In 1915 the government, wishing to control excessive drinking and unruly behaviour in militarily sensitive areas (Lloyd George had said, 'Drink is doing more damage than all the German submarines put together'), took over the management of pubs in several places, the most notable being Carlisle, the centre of many munitions factories, and around Invergordon, an important base of the Home Fleet. Davy often brought with him to Balconie his son Hamish ('Tootie'), then a hyperactive, often irritating but also very funny teenager. He later joined the police and was one of the posse which raided Doug's house looking for drugs; they took possession of a suspicious oily substance in silver paper – which proved to be the remains of a smoked mackerel!

Davy kept coming to Balconie when I fished it, and he and Hamish later took the fishing on the Crown Cairn. We used to watch them in the distance when we fished the bank – near enough to see when they had a shot, but too far away to communicate or tell how many fish they were getting. They kept their boat – a big old coble with an inboard engine – at the RAF camp and motored across the bay to the cairn. One morning, when there were plenty fish going, we saw them leave the cairn in the middle of the tide and head home at top speed. It was obvious that something had gone wrong, and later we discovered that Davy had had a heart attack. I believe he was dead before

Not what it seems. The constable is asking Doug about a net that was stolen from us, while (L to R) Stan, Eddie and Paul M look on. (*ES*)

they got to shore. A few years later, when we were fishing Kiltearn, we witnessed another tragedy on the water. Some time before low water, on a big tide, we spotted the lifeboat coming up from Invergordon. It passed us at top speed, then we watched it slow down as it approached the bridge. Only later did we find out what had happened. One of the fishers on a station above the bridge had fallen into deep water and been taken by the strong current. Wearing waders, he was unable to swim or keep his head above water.

Another of the regulars at the bothy was Bob. The object of considerable envy by Buller ('The man's got three pensions – army, forestry *and* he'll get the OAP'), he was a sly character with a wonderful turn of phrase, greatly enhanced by his slight stammer. Of a rather effeminate acquaintance: 'I don't know if he'd rather g-g-give it or take it.' Of another pal with a large wife: 'Did he take the heavy plant with him?' Of a recently widowed but comely lady in late middle age: 'Aye, there's a good bit o' work in her yet.' Bob was a poacher at heart; he relished the fact that he was able to take an occasional laird's fish away with him from Balconie, and he also had many a fish himself, unofficially, out of the Alness. When Eddie took over at Ardross Castle, he was absolutely spot-on in recommending Bob to mind the Castle's stretch of river. 'I never pay more than £100 for a car', Bob advised me once, 'and when she's done I just put her over the dyke.' This would have been one of those vehicles which the *Ross-shire Journal* in times gone by advertised in the spring and early summer as a 'good holiday car'.

It was at the bothy that I had my first taste of whisky. I'm not sure who took it down, but it was probably Bob, since this was the 'white stuff', in other words the fresh product before it was diluted or barrelled and which had left the distillery by the back door. You couldn't possibly drink this on its own, so the practice was to mix it with undiluted orange squash. The kick was there, but little or no whisky flavour. I would choke some down in an effort to prove my virility, but I thought it was disgusting. Black Heart rum was our spirit of choice in the Balconie Babes days, and it was only gradually that I acquired the taste for the proper thing.

In truth, there were long stretches of boredom in those early days. Apart from Hamish, who was a crucial few years too young for me, there was rarely anybody there under fifty. With

Corporal Bob. (*Gray family*)

Buller on the job, there was no real need for anyone else to watch the water, and even at the height of a good season an hour could easily pass with no action at all. It was only when I came to be a skipper myself that I really discovered the joys of water-watching. Quite apart from the expectation, never extinguished even at the leanest of times, that fish will show, there is the water itself in all its guises, from flat calm (not good for fishing except in the very early morning, because fish are loath to swim into shallow

'A nice steady ripple'. (*JH*)

water without some wind) to lumpy calm (devilish difficult to see fish) to a nice steady ripple, perfect water for fishing, through stiffer breezes and finally a half gale which stirs up the mud and in which the boat bucks and drags her anchor and we start thinking about packing it in and going home. Wind against tide, or a changeable wind, are apt to create jabble on the surface which is often so like the mark of fish that seeing him in it is impossible.

The last season I fished with Buller at Balconie was in my final university vacation (the first time around). I see from my records that it was a good season – about 1,500 fish – and nothing much had changed; the same faces showed up at the bothy – Davy, Bob and the rest; Mary still did the cooking and brewed endless cups of tea; the boat got another coat of pitch, and the net was spread and mended every Saturday morning at the end of the fishing week. But change was in the air. Oil had been discovered in the North Sea, and the firth

Jan.

and its surroundings were about to undergo a transformation. Highland Fabricators were building the rig yard at Nigg which would employ 5,000 people, and the aluminium smelter at Invergordon, which employed another thousand, was soon to begin production. None of this directly impacted the fishing, but it was the end of the age of rural innocence for the eastern half of the county: new roads and bridges were built; new housing estates sprang up, and incomers, many from the Central Belt, flocked to the area; novel foods like avocados and green peppers appeared in the local shops; Inverness became a mini-metropolis.

And it was the end of fishing for me, for the time being. I got a job in advertising in London and then moved to Amsterdam. I also got married. But after seven years I realized that I had to answer the question posed by one of its gurus, 'Is advertising a trade an honest man can engage in?' with a definite 'No'. It was the early years of the green movement, the idea of a self-sufficient life in the country had become very attractive, and I knew there would be a job at the fishing for at least some of the year. So Jan, my wife, and I moved to the Highlands. When I told her that I was going to the fishing, she became rather alarmed, envisaging a trawler and weeks away on dangerous and stormy seas. I reassured her that we never went more than a hundred yards from shore, and although she never became a fisher herself she likes to row and often visited the bothy, on one memorable day bringing champagne and home-made éclairs to celebrate the catching of our 2,000th fish for the season.

12

The Firth

The Cromarty Firth … a highway and a provider.
Marinell Ash, *This Noble Harbour*

Cromarty. To most southern ears just a name on the shipping forecast. Viking, Forties, Cromarty, faraway northern regions suffering gales, poor visibility or 'precipitation in sight'. But the Cromarty Firth is quite a different matter. At its eastern end, this arm of the North Sea is a wide, safe harbour, surrounded by low-lying farmland and protected by two matching headlands known as the Sutors (shoemakers), because they seem to resemble two such craftsmen bent over their lasts. Another local legend has it that they are giants turned to stone and condemned to guard the entrance to the firth in perpetuity. The southern Sutor shelters the little town of Cromarty, the northern, the village and oil rig yard of Nigg. This is the maritime part of the firth – deep, open water where, despite the protection of the Sutors, you can feel the ocean's swell when there is a gale out at sea.

But as the firth extends westward and penetrates the hills it becomes narrower and more placid. Visitors seeing it for the first time, especially if they come from wider lands, often miscall it a river, and so it sometimes seems, when the water is calm and a big ebb is pulling it eastwards to the sea. From the north shore, the green swell of the

Looking out over the outer firth to the Sutors.

The inner firth. Kiltearn and Balconie Point jut out into the water at the left of the photograph.

Black Isle is barely half a mile away, and all along this shore are the fishing stations I know so well: Alness, the Crown Cairn, Balconie, Kiltearn and Foulis. This is the shore where I fished the summers for fifty years.

In effect, there are two firths. The outer part has long been recognized as one of Britain's great natural harbours. To the Vikings, whose realm once included Easter Ross, the firth was *Sykkersand*, or 'Safe Sand'; this will have been the wide, shallow expanse of Nigg Bay. In 1653 Sir Thomas Urquhart, the eccentric laird of Cromarty (his translation of Rabelais' bawdy tales was said to be 'more Rabelaisian than Rabelais himself' and he reportedly died laughing at the news of Charles II's restoration) wrote:

> This harbour, in all the Latine maps of Scotland is called *Portus salutis* [the harbour of safety]; by reason that ten thousand ships together may ride within it in the greatest tempest that is, as in a calm.

Half a century later, Daniel Defoe called it 'the finest harbour, with the least business of, perhaps, any in Britain'. And in 1790, by which time rather more 'business' in the form of shipping had come to the firth, the minister of Cromarty declared:

> Such is the vast extent of sea room in this bay, and such the capacious description of its length, depth and breadth, that almost the whole British navy might, with the greatest safety, ride within view of [Cromarty].

Just over a century later, his words proved prophetic. Admiral 'Jacky' Fisher, First Sea Lord in the Edwardian era and the man responsible for building the first Dreadnought

A calm day on the firth, with oil rigs. (*JH*)

battleship, favoured the use of the firth – 'I've always been dead on for Cromarty', he said – and between the First World War and the 1950s it was an important naval base, although shore facilities were centred not on Cromarty but at Invergordon. Twelve ships sailed from the firth to take part in the Battle of Jutland in 1916.

Visits by the fleet were very valuable to local traders and the source of much local excitement, and there was great dismay when they ceased in the 1950s. Nowadays, the battleships have been replaced by cruise liners, and Invergordon's wide main street is no longer, as a resident described it once to me, 'just a sea of blue from the sailors' jackets'. I can remember seeing some naval vessels in the firth, and as a teenager I encountered a relic of those days. Donsie the butcher, a rogue if ever there was one and a great favourite of my mother's, took me for an illegal (I was under age) drink in Invergordon and offered to set me up with a 'girl'. She proved to be an elderly prostitute who in better days had serviced the fleet, and as the tabloids used to say, I 'made an excuse and left'. She might have been the lady known locally as 'The Beetle' – because she 'lay on her back and waved her legs in the air'!

When I was at the fishing with Buller in the 1960s there was little industrial activity on the firth. But this wasn't to last. The aluminium smelter at Invergordon built a new pier and started production in 1971. Then came North Sea oil and a rush to develop sites inside this perfect base for exploitation of the new fields. In the early 1970s the 'largest man-made hole in Europe' was dug at Nigg – a dock for the construction of oil rigs. At Balconie we regularly salvaged scaffold boards which floated up the firth from Nigg and put them to use around the bothy.

Toasting the season's first fish with Buller at Alness. (*Black family*)

he old bothy, with
he Corsican pines in
he background.

Watching the water, Dagger Gordon and self. (*JH*)

The Balconie Babes. (L to R) Eddie, Stevie, self. (*DM*)

The Balconie bothy. (*FC*)

The Black Isle, looking green. (*JH*)

'Lumpy calm'. (*JH*)

The net comes in. (*DM*)

Senior fishermen. (L to R) Eddie, Rik, Stevie Web, self. (*JH*)

Back from the bank with a load of fish. Eddie and Stevie Web boxing them. (*DM*)

A bunch of 'donkeys'. (*DM*)

Piling the net, self and Eddie. (*ES*)

Rod and self. (*JH*)

Long-rope men at Kiltearn. Rik and self. (*JH*)

Jan on the oars with Steve K (left) and Eddie.

Fish have been spotted – Rod and I set off for a shot on the last day that we ever fished. (*Robert Blake*)

The Firthland is famous for its rainbows.

'Doug and George at the Fishing'.
(*Painting by Ingebjorg Smith*)

Two for the pot. A grilsie and a nice sea trout.

A July dawn on the firth.

Rod working on the net.

Looking across the musselbanks to the Black Isle. (*JH*)

The 'Estate pirates' in later years
– Eddie and self. (*Robert Blake*)

'Lifting the Anchor'. (*Painting by Robert Blake*)

Setting off for the
sandbank. (*DM*)

At the same time, there was a fever of speculative plans for all sorts of oil-related development along the whole north shore of the firth. The tide tables for the firth, published by the Port Authority, carry to this day a statement that the Authority is empowered to 'develop land … in the vicinity of Balconie Point'. We used to worry about this, but like so many schemes around the firth, nothing has ever materialized. A sandbank in Nigg Bay which was ripe for reclamation was sold for £50,000 in 1976 and re-sold for £600,000 the next year as a possible base for an ethylene plant. It never got built. Neither did a projected oil refinery and petrochemical complex at Nigg or a concrete platform yard at Alness. The aluminium smelter closed in 1981, a great blow to the area and yet another example of the industrial boom and bust which has long afflicted the Highlands. Today, there is an oil terminal and work in the renewable energy sector at Nigg, and a newish pier which crosses the Balconie sandbank and carries pipeline fabricated on the Highland Deephaven Industrial Estate to the *Apache* pipe-laying ship. Oil rigs are inspected, repaired and maintained in Invergordon and at Nigg, and the firth shelters a good many rigs, parked while they wait for repair or for the tugs to come and take them back to work; some appear in the photographs in this book. But, thank goodness, the firth has never seen what was once envisaged as its future: a linear city all the way along the north shore, and full-scale industrial development along with it.

*   *   *

The firth owes its shape to the last ice age, when a glacier scoured out an enormous trench, then cut through a mountain range, leaving the Sutors on each side of the gap. Some 12,000 years ago, the ice melted and the land rose, leaving raised beaches around the firth, some of which are now exploited for their sand and gravel. In one such, on the Black Isle opposite Balconie, is some of the earliest evidence of man around the firth: a Stone Age midden of discarded shells.

The shellfish of the firth have been exploited since earliest times. Mussel beds are recorded as being worked in the fifteenth century, and for a long time oysters were also fished. In 1883 and 1884 over 50,000 oysters were landed in Cromarty, but today all we see are empty shells – the legacy of over-fishing in the nineteenth century and perhaps of disease. However, it has recently been announced that oyster farming is coming to the firth.

Salmon have been exported from here since at least the fifteenth century, and the salmon fishings in and around the Conon were historically a very valuable asset, as were the nets in the Alness and Balconie area. The Conon river system is the largest north of the Great Glen; as well as the main river there are four substantial tributaries, and the system enjoys a big run of fish. In the later nineteenth century, although 'fixed engines' had been banned inside the Sutors, there were still net and coble stations in the firth and in the Conon itself, as well as cruives in the river. In 1895 the nets in the district caught 27,200 fish. In 1907, 150 'clean fish' (i.e. not kelts) were caught in the first sweep on 11 February, the opening day of the season (I would have loved to see that – imagine all those big springers!), and in 1909 it was reported that twenty-seven nets were operated in just three and a quarter miles of water. This level of exploitation concerned the proprietors of rod fishings, and in 1920 a number of them formed the Moray Firth Salmon Fishing Company to buy fishing rights and control the operation of the nets. The nets in the lower reaches of the Conon, on which Buller worked between the wars, continued to be very productive – between 1977 and 1986 their annual average catch was close to 2,000 fish. But as numbers began to dwindle in the 1980s, the netting effort was gradually reduced, and in 1991 the rights were bought by the Atlantic Salmon Conservation Trust and the station closed down.

Cromarty was always the most active fishing port of the firth, although most of its fishermen's operations took place outside the firth itself, in the Moray Firth or further afield. The herring fishery was particularly important, although it was notoriously subject to booms and busts: there would be a run of good years, and then the herring would disappear, for no apparent reason. Occasionally they would come into the firth itself, as in the autumn of 1780:

> A body of herrings was seen betwixt the Sutors, swimming up the frith [*sic*, a common spelling in earlier times] with all the accompaniments of a large shoal, whales, porpoises and seagulls.

The fish got as far as Ardullie, well into the inner firth, where they were 'fished in immense quantities within four hundred yards of the shore.' I wish I had been there to see it. Apart from ourselves, the only commercial fishing I have ever seen in the firth was when, back in the 1970s and 80s, a few purse-seine boats came in after Kessock herring and sprats. We shall not see these again, because since 2004 'fishing for sea fish with a trawl, Danish seine or similar net, purse seine, ring net or dredge (including a suction dredge) [has been] prohibited within the areas within Scottish inshore waters specified …' and these include the firth.

The last relics of the local herring fishery can still just be seen at low water on Foulis and Ardullie Points. Here the herring fishermen who left for the war in 1914 beached their 'Zulu' boats; many of the men did not return, and the boats were never re-floated. I can recall the skeletons of several being quite intact, but now the action of wind and tide has reduced them to a few scraps.

Many of the fishermen who manned the Zulus came not from Cromarty but from the 'seaboard' villages, Hilton, Balintore and Shandwick, outside the firth, where a distinctive culture and way of life persisted until very recently. Edwin Chadwick, the great Victorian social reformer, in his *Report on the sanitary condition of the labouring population in Scotland* concluded that 'intermarriages [of fisherfolk] with the rural populations are very uncommon' – 'Cod and corn dinna mix', as the local saying had it. In small fishing communities this could result in a dangerous degree of in-breeding. My mother's doctor, whose practice was chiefly in the seaboard area, once told her that in the early years of the twentieth century she had attended a good many 'monstrous births', as she called them.

* * *

The firthland is a curious hybrid of a place. The firth itself is surrounded by an agricultural landscape which is distinctly lowland in character, but it is backed by Highland hills, notably the great bulk of Ben Wyvis, more than 1,000m in height. The seaboard villages and the farming country of the Tarbat peninsula have much in common with the Moray coast or Aberdeenshire, whereas Dingwall, at the head of the firth, is more Highland in character, serving a central and western hinterland. It's not uncommon to see in the Dingwall shops a shepherd or a stalker in tweeds, the kind of figure you rarely meet in Alness or Invergordon.

And so much has changed in the last fifty years or so. The local accent has altered in my lifetime; it is relatively rare to hear a pure Ross-shire voice nowadays, except from older folk, many of today's residents having a tinge of Inverness or Glasgow in their speech. The oil-related developments of the 1970s brought people to the area from the Central Belt and from England, and many of them have stayed. The place is a great deal busier. There is even a substantial rush hour in and out of Inverness.

Culturally and socially, the firthland has a mix of the careful, flinty attitudes of the North-East and the gentler, more casual habits of the Highlands and the West. Its special charm is that it cannot be pigeon-holed. My cousin Hector Munro, who has known it all his life, once said to me that he saw it as a kind of island – water on one side and the wilderness on the other, with just a couple of routes out at either end. It is somehow symptomatic that the Gulf Stream, which bathes the shores of the western Highlands, licks round the top of Scotland and reaches the firthland, but there it stops.

The firth seen from the Fyrish monument. (*Gina Chamier*)

13

Diaries

For a few years I kept a diary of the fishing, recording weather, fish caught and notable events. Eventually, this became little more than numbers jotted against the relevant day in my tide book, but the earlier entries can be entertaining: *15 May* 'Bedstead in the net at the Blue House'; *28 July* 'One blank with the Jonah in pebble glasses'; *23 June* 'Perfect conditions and not a bloody thing to be seen. A blank at mullet. Plants eaten by slugs. A bad day'; *11 August* [a Saturday] 'Gale blew up. Off to Donsie, Tain and hotels [to sell fish]. Free pint and a feel at the Morangie'; *29 June* 'Shot of eleven. Jubilation, grilse and wine for lunch'. And some of the numbers make remarkable reading – did we really catch that many fish?

There are quite a few mentions of 'plants', occasionally coded as 'friends'. These were, of course, marijuana plants, set discreetly along the old fence line at the back of the trees behind the bothy and protected from rabbits with scraps of wire netting. Quite apart from the damage caused by slugs, they did not really flourish in the sandy soil of the Point, nor were they as well hidden as we imagined. An elderly couple, sent down one day by somebody to 'watch the fishermen' (this sort of visit was an occasional hazard) and realizing they were not completely welcome, set off for a walk. When they returned, the husband – I have a feeling he may have been a retired admiral – said, 'I spotted your lupins growing at the back there.' Luckily he was no botanist – although the leaves are quite similar – but 'lupins' they remained to us ever after.

Birds appear regularly: *9 June* 'Swallows' first egg' – for several years we hosted a pair in the goat shed next to the bothy. On *22 June* 'Swan hatched two' – a pair of mute swans nested for many years on the extreme east end of

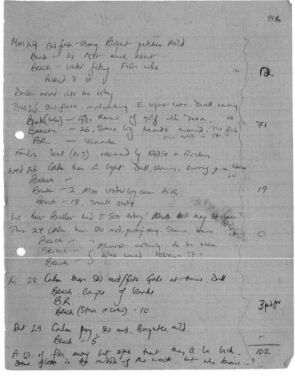

A July week (not a very good one) from my diary.

the Point, as did a small colony of common terns. But ever since the Skiach was bridged and the shore path became a fairway for dog-walkers, all the ground-nesting birds – terns, ringed plovers, oystercatchers, common sandpipers, skylarks, meadow pipits – which used to breed here have gone.

On *3 June* 'Took swan's egg on the way in.' This records a strange incident. On the way back from the bank we saw a pair of swans busy heaping up a pile of weed halfway down the ebb, and it became apparent that this was their 'nest'. They were clearly an inexperienced pair, and the pen must have been desperate to lay. As the tide got closer to the nest, their efforts to shore it up became ever more frantic, until it was almost under water. I waded out to it, the birds made off and I found that the nest contained a single egg, which I took, knowing it had to be completely fresh and would

My biggest fish (29lbs).

otherwise soon float away. Later in the day, Jan and I went for a walk on the hill behind Achandunie and found some fungi which we identified as St George's mushrooms, one of the few edible species which fruit in spring and summer rather than autumn. That evening, we congratulated ourselves on being the only people in the world to be sitting down to a meal of scrambled swan's egg and fried St George's mushrooms. The mushrooms were excellent, but egg was very dark orange and so strong-tasting as to be barely edible.

On *11 August* 'Saw the fish of the century. 50lbs?' To be strictly accurate, I did not see this fish. The Balconie Babes were out on the bank, Eddie and Stevie watching upwind while I watched the other way. Suddenly there was a big splash behind me and volley of astonished shouts from the lads, and I whipped round.

'That was a monster! Go for it!'

I could see the mark of a jump, fairly well out though not too far, but I couldn't see him swimming – there was a fair breeze blowing and the water off the bank is deep. But we had to have a go, so we rowed a good wide shot, trying to time him. Of course, it was a blank ('You're getting greedy', Buller would have said). The crew had a pretty good eye for fish by this time and they swore they had never seen anything nearly as big. Now the Conon record fish on the rod is only about 33lbs, and I have never heard of an Alness fish reaching that size; the biggest fish I ever saw out of the firth was 29lbs; and Buller himself never saw one over 30lbs. But fish from other local rivers may well enter the firth at times, and the Ness certainly contains big fish – the media got very excited a few years ago about the 'REAL Loch Ness monster', claimed to be two inches longer than the British record rod-caught fish of 64lbs. But was our 'fish of the century' really 50lbs? I doubt it. Maybe forty, though …

Early in the season, rather than record individual days, on many of which not a lot happened, I would write a summary of the first few weeks. Here is a typical one:

Got started with Buller in the second week of May. Fish were in the river in late April and we may have missed a small early run. Only twelve for May at Alness but we did see fish fairly regularly and had several blanks – including one at a really good-looking head in the last week of the month. I had the bank in front of the Big Cairn pushed up, also the tractor cairn. Eddie arrived at the end of the month and we had the first day's fishing at Balconie on 1 June. Dave and Rik are making another (small) net and have constructed a fine new bothy [on Balachladdich beach]. The Balconie bothy has suffered again (shotgun wounds this time). Fine, hot, sunny weather.

In the nature of things, many of the diary entries comment on how the season is going. Quite often, things are not going that well: *1 July* 'Fish scarce and wide. Great gloom' [this was a Monday, usually a good day, and after quite a few fish had been seen the week before]; *12 July* 'Fucking N wind again. No fishing'; *5 August* [in a very poor, wet season] 'Good head in the net, but ground rope over the top. Slept gloomily. Nothing to be seen. The nadir.' It's not all gloom, however: *2 August* 'Suddenly the fish are back. Good size too' [this in a season when, unusually, the first fortnight of August saw the best catches]; *28 June* 'Buller had 30 [at Alness] this evening. Are they on?' *2 July* [at the bank] '19, including a 12 for the bottle [this was a bet]. Still some biggies. A great morning.'

Some of the most evocative entries are from the beginning and end of the season. On *4 June* 'First fish eaten by Achandunie house and cottage and guests at Tim's christening [it must have been a big one]. A lucky shot at an unlucky jumper. Pitched the boat thoroughly.'

At the end of one season, Eddie and I were sent up to try a shot in Loch Morie at the head of the Alness river. The Estate had the right to use a net there, and if the right was not exercised it might lapse. Anticipating nothing but trouble – the bed of the loch would probably be covered in all sorts of snags which could do untold damage to the net – we found a bay that looked reasonably clean and I rowed a wide shot round it. We pulled the net in, thankful that we had not connected with any tree trunks but not expecting anything else, when, blow me down, there was a fish in it. It was a large black thing, not very lively, and I reckoned it was a very stale salmon which had been in the loch since spring. But no, scale analysis showed that it was a 13¾lb brown trout, a *ferox* (cannibal fish); these usually live in deep water in the daytime, so the fact that it was swimming around in a shallow bay suggests it wasn't in the best of health. Stuffed, mounted and prettified, it was displayed in the Estate office, where anglers came to get permits for the loch. They would have been very lucky ever to see a trout of that size.

A more typical week at the end of the season passed like this: 'Calm days, some sun, some rain, very few fish. Cut wood, went visiting. Cricket and idling.'

14

A Couple of Good Weeks

In the entries below from my diaries, the numbers represent fish caught on each tide (if in brackets, they refer to individual shots). The figures in bold are the declared catch for the day or week. Some simple arithmetic will tell you that not all the fish went off to market.

In these busy weeks we fished three tides a day, which meant being there from first light (not long after 4.00 am in July) till dusk (around 10.00 pm). Of course, there were breaks between tides when we had the boat out of the water and ate, or sometimes had a kip – and some fishers (I'm thinking of Eddie in particular) could even snatch forty winks in the boat or on the cairn when not much was happening. Occasionally I took a tide off, and these are recorded, e.g. Thur 20 in the first week below, when the crew (Eddie and Stevie) fished the morning tide.

At this date the fishing week, by law, was from 6.00 am on Monday morning to midday on Saturday (later amended to 6.00 pm Friday). Monday was usually the best day, since fish would have had a couple of days to collect, but Saturday mornings, funnily enough, were often very productive. Here's the record of one Saturday on which we managed to fish two tides (although the boat must have come out well before the end of high water):

Sat 21 Variable, light. Dull, showers   **176**
Bank – 126. Never stopped. No time for the piece
Shot of 51 in the water
Beach – 57
An incredible morning

The diaries are sprinkled with days when things went awry – 'Bloody north wind again'; 'Good head in the net and the ground rope went over the floats'; 'Thunder, rain and spate'; 'Arrived late and angry'; 'No fish. Great gloom'. But sometimes things went well. The weeks below are from July in two different years.

Mon 17 W light–mod. Showers. Warm   **115**
Beach – 98 (33, 28, 20 etc.) Great stuff
Bank – 13 Fish fairly scarce
Beach – 5 A beautiful evening

Tues 18 W/NW light–mod. Dull   **115**
Beach – 35 (small shots)
Bank – 50 (27 & 21)
Beach – 31 (one shot)
Slept in the bothy

Wed 19 SW, going N. Dull   **34**
Bank – 20
Beach – 9 Strong wind, dirty water
Musselbank – 8, then Bank – 1 Wind too north
Blanks. Plenty fish around. One trout

Thur 20 Calm, going NNE mod. Brighter. Cool   **132**
Bank – 29 (crew)
Beach – 94 (incl. 45)
Bank – 24, 2 trout. All jumpers. Never got into them right, but plenty
fish around
Slept in the bothy. Extra good trout for dinner

Fri 21 Calm, going SW mod. Dull, drizzly, warm   **100**
Bank – 93 (big shots)   **20**
Beach – 7 Big tides not so good at the beach
Rover stuck in the ford
Bank – 25, 1 mullet
Tesa arrived

Sat 22 Calm, then SW strong. Dull, showery, warm   **41**
Bank – 27 Never really got into them. Biggest ebb of the season
Beach – 15

A fantastic week. One more like it and … [in fact, there was rain over the
weekend, and we only got just over 100 the next week]   **557**

The following week is from a different year:

Mon 23 W light, going N. Dull, cool   **192**
Bank – 99 Loads of fish, big heads (incl. 51)
Beach – 93 And again
B/Rock, Musselbank, Bank – 8 With Doug, John and Steve. A terrible night,
fish playing us up. Four blanks

Tues 24 Calm, going E light. Dull, close   **191**
Bank – 187 (incl. 62). All big shots. Amazing
Beach – 19. Not much about
Musselbank/Bank – 10. With Doug. Very little to be seen, but a fine,
gentle night

Wed 25 Calm, going E. Close, some sun, some rain   **120**
Bank – 41 (crew)
Beach – 59. With Wilf
Skiach – 22. With Doug. Too calm for it, but loads of fish around
A lovely night

Thur 26 Calm, going E light. Warm, mostly dull   **148**
Bank – 110. Loads of fish about. Big shots. Two beautiful trout
Beach – 18. With Wilf
Musselbank – 23. With Steve and Doug. Another fine night
Drunken John Major at the bothy [not the former Prime Minister]

Fri 27 W light, going E light. Dull, warm   **97**
Bank – 77 (smaller shots)
Beach – 2 Plenty around, but fish made fools of us. Anthony visited
Dogfight
Musselbank (Ed and Doug) – 20

Sat 28 E light, then calm. Dull and warm   **26**
Bank – 31 Not so much about

Just amazing, but signs that they're taking off. It surely can't go on.   **764**
[The previous week, we had had over 500, but right enough, there was a
small spate and we only got 117 the next week]

15

A July Morning

Around midsummer in the Highlands it is never fully dark. The sun is only hiding below the line of hills to the north, and at 3.30 am there is plenty light to see what you are doing, if not yet quite enough to see fish. The air is still this morning, apart from a gentle offshore waft which brings with it the growthy scent of ripening barley. The fishers should have been up and doing, making tea and getting ready for the morning tide – low water is not long after six, it's a big tide and they will be making for the sandbank. But there are no signs of life from the bothy.

Then down the track comes Alan. He hammers on the bothy door.

'Wake up, you idle bastards!'

On the sandbank. (*RR*)

The skipper throws off his sleeping bag, prods his mate awake and the two of them stumble around the bothy, pulling on boots and filling a flask of coffee. This is Saturday, and it has been a long week. Leaving them to it, Alan walks impatiently over to the grey Fergie, pulls the starting handle out of its holster and cranks her into life. Finally, crew, piece-bags and oilskins are ready, the skipper climbs aboard the tractor and they set off, towing the boat down the beach and across the ebb towards the mouth of the Black Rock river. There's a handy deep pool near the edge, and the skipper turns the tractor and reverses the trailer into it, while the crew slide the boat off. Then he drives the tractor and trailer fifty yards or so back up towards the beach and parks her on a ridge of sand and stones. By the time he gets back, the crew have set the oars on their pins and walked the boat down the river channel to salt water. They all climb in, the skipper takes the bow oars, the crew a stern oar each, and they set off for the sandbank, a quarter of a mile away. It's an easy row going with the tide in the calm water.

Halfway to the bank there is the sound of a couple of splashes ahead, and everyone turns round. There's a head coming out of the deep, and my God, what a head! – a great broad swim, the water shaking like crazy on either side as he passes over a musselbank. And behind it there's another, and then another, just as good. The firth is full of fish; there could be several hundred in sight right now. The crew, keen to get to work, bend to their oars and soon pass the halfway cairns, the Blimp, the Pimple and the Tangle.

By the time they arrive, the bank is well up. It's a half-mile strip of sand, punctuated at its west end by the stones of an old cairn and in the east by a patch of lacers, then the Crown Cairn, and nowadays the pipeline pier. Buller used to send me down with a huik (sickle) to cut the lacers, which he called 'sea ware'. Behind is a lagoon of shallow water, so although the bank is an extension of the ebb, it seems as if you are on an island. It's a wonderful place to fish. The water is clean and deep, and wanderers often turn up from further afield – Arctic skuas a couple of times, twisting in

A foggy morning on the bank. Stevie has just spotted fish and is lifting the anchor. (*DM*)

the air like gigantic swallows, and once a great skua, a bonxie, down from Orkney to harass the local gulls.

When porpoises were still common – before the bottlenose dolphin pod arrived and drove them away or killed them – they were a frequent sight off the bank. One morning long ago, I was fishing there with Buller. He and Pattie were in the boat, and I was on the bank with the rope. A good head was spotted coming nicely along the shoreline, Buller lifted the anchor and I picked up the rope. I had pulled a few feet of net off the boat when there came an agonized shout: 'Drop your rope! Drop your rope!' A bit bewildered, I did as I was told, although it seemed we were about to miss a good head. But Buller had spotted something different about the swim, and a few seconds later a sleek black back surfaced briefly before ducking under the rope and away. Buller knew from bitter experience that a porpoise will make an awful mess of your net.

This morning, it's a busy tide. Shot after shot, and the pile of fish on the sand grows steadily, covered in seaweed to keep them moist and cool as the sun comes up. Every now and again, we pour a bailer-full of water over them. The bailer is a 5-litre plastic bottle with the top cut off – the perfect flexible shape to scoop water out of the curved

Boxing a big catch. (*DM*)

bottom of a boat. There are no really big shots, but then again, off the bank the water is so deep that fish don't always show well, and it's difficult to tell what a shot is going to be; even a really good head may sometimes put up very little water. There is a lull just before low water, time to get out the flask and the piece – cheese and chutney baps, made the night before to save time in the morning – and for the mate to roll a joint and pass it round. Then it's action again, as the tide turns and fish begin to come back towards the bank from the west.

Finally, it's time to go. The bank is beginning to disappear as the tide gets a grip, and the crew start getting the fish on board, giving each a quick dip to wash the sand off. First they lay fish out of the way, under the backboard and in the bow, but these places fill up, and pretty soon the whole bottom of the boat is covered in silver. It has been a three-figure tide, and as they row home, the coble is perceptibly lower in the water laden as she is with a quarter of a ton of fish. It is just as well that there is little wind; it is not unknown to have to walk the boat home from the bank if a gale gets up during the tide.

Rather than load this weight on to the trailer, the skipper climbs out at the mouth of the Black Rock to fetch the tractor, while the crew row round the Big Cairn to the front of the bothy. The skipper carefully arranges seven empty boxes on the trailer and backs it gently down the beach to meet the incoming boat. Boxing the fish takes a while – they swill each in the water again, then pack them side by side on their backs. Once a box is full, it is washed a final time in the sea, then balanced across the framework of scaffold poles which make up the body of the trailer and towed up the beach.

The boxes safely in the lean-to and the anchor pulled right up the beach, the crew set about making breakfast. As the tide begins to fill, there is usually a fish or two which noses in to explore the shoreline in front of the bothy. But the crew pay these no attention. The water is still shallow and weedy, coffee and bacon and eggs are coming and there will be plenty time to deal with these guys at high water. It's been a very good morning.

16

At the Fishing

George Huntley

This poem records a trip to the sandbank.

The wind's against us & it's quite a pull
the scalloped water gurgling at each stroke;
in a daze, a dream, the oars dip in & thrust,

the rowlocks squeak & rattle,
but we hardly seem to move:
light spray blows off the wavecrests like a drizzle
as we bend our backs & straighten, bend again
& time slows down, & thought becomes a circle,
each breath aware of nothing but the moment

then looking up you see with some surprise
we have been making progress
& the battered old tractor
we left back on the shore
already in a quarter of an hour
has receded, shrinking down
to the size of a toy, a small grey bullock
waiting by some distant trees
for our return

& soon enough way out upon the water
though the wind's against us & it's quite a pull
we reach our destination:
one of those sandbanks
that uplift themselves
on an ebbing tide
in the middle of the firth;
we rest on our oars,
as the keel grates onto pebbles,

jump out into the shallows
of this unknown world

& here for the next few hours
is our fishing station,
a broad expanse of drying sand & gravel,
littered with purple mussel-shells,
with wave-wet stones & seaweed
& the scattered limbs of little orange crabs,
a temporary island;
& here in the briskness of the sun,
the scurrying breeze,
we'll watch & wait;
but first of all the rituals of the morning
– a tern passing above us, with its jerky flight –
Who's got a light? in my cupped hands

A blowy day at the bank. (*RR*)

the shaky flame, the blue smoke of a roll-up
& where's the coffee? from a thermos safely wedged
among the rocks
we pour a mug & share its blessing round

then down to business, in the weather's eye,
two on the boat & two ashore
rope loosely linked between us,
as we gaze out on the water's endless motion
each trying to interpret what it says;
an ancient scene of chance & skill
for somewhere in that mass of jumbled waves
the noble fish are swimming up the firth
like slow torpedoes nosing to their mark
from the open sea back to their birthing rivers;
we wait alert as herons
(even as we joke & talk)
for the slightest trace of those incoming ripples;
on the stern of the boat our sweep-net
ready-poised
at the first great shout
to fling its dripping folds across their path ...

17

At Alness

'Alness – such a mess!' sang The Tools, a local punk outfit, in 1977. And even before industry came to Ross-shire in the late 1960s and the population of Alness doubled in just three years, bringing many social problems, it always had the reputation of being a scruffy, slightly dodgy village. Underneath its changed face – the Glaswegian accents in the street, the big supermarkets, the whey-faced guys waiting outside the chemist's for their methadone prescriptions, as well as the many wins in Britain in Bloom and Scotland in Bloom competitions – elements of the old place can still be seen: the fine sandstone bank building, two traditional butcher's shops and the Dalmore distillery. It was at the last of these, just outside the town beside the firth, that we kept our boats when we fished the Alness station.

We had connections there. The manager of the distillery was a pal of Stan's (he got a few fish every season, of course), and Paul the Pole was still working there as a

The Yankee Pier in early morning. (*RR*)

mashman, responsible for turning the malted barley into 'wort' (the liquid extracted in the mashing process) and then 'wash' (the finished product of fermentation before it is distilled). Paul and Aggie lived in a tied house at the distillery, and we kept boat and net, tractor and trailer, and a big pile of fish boxes near their place, but hidden away behind a storage shed containing many hundreds of barrels of maturing whisky. You wouldn't want these fish boxes too close to your house, anyway – they get pretty ripe in warm weather.

We would tow the boat with the tractor out of the distillery and on to the beginning of the Yankee Pier, then down across the ebb and out to the fishing cairns. The pier is so called because it dates from the time when the US Navy took over the distillery during the Great War as a mine base. In the 1930s the RAF used Alness as a training site for

Heading home from the Alness cairns. Doug driving, Gary kneeling, Paul sitting. (*RR*)

flying boats, first Saro Londons and Stranraers, then in October 1939 a squadron of Sunderlands and Catalinas. The RAF station was still in existence when we were fishing, and the Crown cairn crew kept their boat at the shore beside it. I have a foggy memory of a drunken night in the mess, when all the fishers gathered there and Stevie Web made off with the squadron's flag.

The fishing at Alness was nearly all at low water. You could fish high tide on the beach to the west of the river mouth if there was a steady east wind blowing – the kind of wind which carries a yeasty odour up the firth from the big distillery at Invergordon – but we rarely caught many fish there. When I took on a share of Alness, Doug and I constructed a basic bothy on the beach, but it didn't last long. We soon discovered that the fishing was hopeless without a good east breeze, and the site was just too easy for vandals from the village to get at.

Eddie described the fishing at Alness to me as 'a bit industrial', and I suppose it was, compared to Balconie. On a standard Balconie day we would fish three tides, picking up sometimes smallish numbers on each until we had a respectable total. At Alness, by contrast, there might only be one tide on some days, and it could be pretty full-on. Mind you, Eddie could have been put off Alness by that day when he and

Doug, fishing there with a leaky old boat, had seven blanks in a row, caught a net full of weed and then got the boat stranded – with Doug's false teeth floating in the bilges; they had shot out when he was straining to pull her off the mud.

The big difference was this: at Balconie and Kiltearn we were fishing near the mouths of two small spate rivers, the Skiach and the Black Rock; neither supports a big run of fish, but both spill fresh water out into the firth, attracting passers-by which are heading for the Conon to the west or have overshot the Alness to the east. At Alness, by contrast, we fished at the mouth of a river (I call it the Alness, but some locals prefer 'Averon') which has a serious run of fish – I have seen estimates that

Paul on Teaninich cairn with a stack of boxes. (*RR*)

this was well over 10,000 at the time we were fishing. Incidentally, this gives some context to the rods/nets controversy; even in our best years the nets never took even half of that, and not all our catch would have been heading for the Alness anyway.

At the height of the run, the numbers of fish at Alness could be pretty impressive. I have seen giant heads go by, just out of reach in the deep water directly off the river mouth, which probably contained well over a hundred fish. Big shots were frequent – I never saw one myself of three figures, but they did occur. There were so many fish that we tended to express our catch not in numbers but in boxes. These were no longer the specialized salmon boxes which hold twenty grilse, but ordinary flat, wooden fish boxes which would take twelve or thirteen. On the busiest tides you needed a big crew, and the action could be relentless. Most fish were caught on the two west-wind cairns, Teaninich and Dalmore (each named after one of the two local distilleries). Dalmore is pretty close to the end of the Yankee Pier, and there seems to be a highway that fish follow, round the end of the pier and straight past the cairns. On the biggest tides, these places got too shallow and we would move to the Cage – named for the metal structure on top of the cairn which allegedly resembled the notorious fixtures in the segregation unit at Porterfield Prison in Inverness. If the wind was in the east, we would fish the Bell and the Little Bell, looking towards the tall pole which once marked the inward limit for big naval ships to anchor safely.

Doug and Paul enjoying a row to the Bell. (*RR*)   Waiting for fish at Alness. Gary smoking, Doug
mending the net. (*RR*)

One year, a lot of untreated sewage was discharged into the firth just to the east
of the beach. This became obvious when crowds of gulls descended on it; you could
smell it sometimes, and unpleasant objects occasionally washed up on the shore. I don't
believe it had any effect on the fishing – it only appeared at high water and did not
come near the areas where we were operating – but I hastily put in an application to
the local authority for compensation, and the resulting sum bumped up our take for
that season considerably. Another potential disturbance came when, one season, some
huge oil rig flotation tanks were cut up on the west side (i.e. facing us) of the Yankee
Pier. There was considerable noise from oxy-acetylene cutting equipment, cranes and
lorries, but it seemed to have absolutely no effect on the fish – just confirming my belief
that very little will deflect them from their single-minded urge to run the river and
breed.

It wasn't generally too difficult to rustle up extra crew for Alness. People knew there
was a good chance of seeing some action, getting a dram and going home with a fish.
In fact, the cairn could get very crowded and a bit noisy some evenings. I know what
Eddie meant by 'industrial'. Of course, it wasn't always like that; there were plenty
of tides, especially early and late in the season, when crews were smaller, things were
much quieter and the essence of fishing was as it ever was: watching the water and the
sky, observing the birds, enjoying the craic – and if a few fish came along, so much
the better.

18

An Evening High Water

The first week of July, and an evening high water on Balconie beach. This June hasn't been great: a lot of north wind, only a very few big fish and a lot of blank tides. But yesterday there were a couple of small shotties of grilse off the Slippery Stones, so hopes are rising. Tonight there is hardly a cloud in the sky, but there is a fresh north-westerly breeze and it is far from warm. The firth seems strangely empty, as it often does when the tide is in. The shore birds, oystercatchers, curlews and redshanks, are somewhere above the tideline waiting for the ebb to uncover their feeding grounds, and the crows and jackdaws which share it with them are away in the fields above. A couple of swans sail off the river mouth, and the odd gull tacks into the wind looking for scraps.

The first mate has gone home, but the skipper and the second mate have hung on, shifting the boat to the east of the point to catch some calmer water. They are sitting in

Looking east over the old coble. Painting by Robert Blake.

the lee of the old coble, which lies high and dry in the grass above the high water mark. She is beginning to fall apart. Her bow and part of the gunwale are still showing, but her stern has disappeared, plundered for kindling for the bothy stove, and her bottom is buried under pebbles and turf.

Then, far off and well out in the channel, the sunlight catches a white plume of spray against the deep blue of the firth. A jumper! Then another, and another. And so it starts. In the next hour or so they see more than a hundred, sometimes just the spray, iridescent in the low sun, but often the full slashing jump of himself, not for nothing called *Salar* – the leaper. There are so many that they soon cease to remark on them. No fish comes close to shore, and they never touch oar or net, but they go home happy. The fish are here.

The Balconie Lady, waiting for action. (*Robert Blake*)

19

East Wind on the Beach

There were days on the Balconie beach when we really didn't need an audience or any distractions. Hard-core fishing tides when the heads piled in one after another, and if we weren't rowing a shot and pulling the net, we were killing and boxing fish.

One of these days coincided with the arrival of some rather unlikely visitors – not that one hadn't been to the fishing before, but she didn't quite fit the bothy ethos. Rather older than us, she was a single lady of literary and artistic tastes, and she had brought along her sister, someone we didn't know at all.

Killing a good shot of fish. (*RR*)

It really wasn't a day for tourists. The clouds were low, the sky was uniformly grey, a cold wind was blowing hard from the east and bringing with it small but penetrating rain. We had had our oilskins on since the beginning of the tide.

I did wonder why they had come, but since they had made the effort to get to the bothy, the least we could do was offer them a cup of tea and a biscuit, and a seat on the east wind bench, where there was some shelter from the wind and the rain. We did not, however, have much time to entertain them, because it was one of those days when the fish kept coming as if on a conveyor belt.

There were no very big shots, but each head would strike up fairly well out, halfway to the Skiach, then home in on the beach and follow it. Every shot moved us slightly further from the bothy, and apart from when we went back to fetch more boxes, we scarcely exchanged a word with our visitors, who by now had taken refuge inside.

Finally there was something of a lull. By now we were almost at the old bothy, too far along the beach in fact, so we walked the boat back. This was when the best head of the day showed up, and we rowed our shot at it directly in front of the bothy. Like every other shot that day, it went perfectly, and we pulled in around twenty fish, including a couple of donkeys. Already high on our previous success, we gave out some wild yells as we pulled the bag on to dry land. Our visitors had emerged from the bothy to watch, and I thought I saw a slightly fearful look cross the face of our friend's sister.

Now, of course, it was killing time. We each took a stick, knelt on the net and began to dispatch the fish. As I hit one of the donkeys a lethal blow on the nose, I looked up towards the bothy. This time there was no mistaking the look on the lady's face; it was one of extreme distaste, and suddenly I saw ourselves through her eyes – three rough and cruel men exulting in the death of these beautiful creatures.

They left soon afterwards.

20

Ardroy

Ardroy – 'Aird', promontory; 'ruadh', red; a point west of Alness Point. The 'stell' or fishing station of Ardroy is mentioned in 1479; also 'the Flukaris croft'.

W. J. Watson, *Place-Names of Ross and Cromarty* (1904)

Astell is the station from which a form of sweep-netting was practised (see Chapter 2, Catching the Fish), and a 'Flukar' is a flounder fisherman. Some maps show 'Ardroy' as the name of the sands in Alness bay.

Doug and self rowing a shot. (*RR*)

This is why I chose the name 'Ardroy Fisheries' for a venture of my own. After a few successful seasons back at Balconie, a half share of the Alness fishings came up for rent and I took it for four years, in partnership with the Brigadier and Stan the forester. The Brigadier would put up the rent, Stan would take care of getting the fish to market, and since the other half of the fishing was owned by the Estate and worked by Buller, it was a simple matter to share some gear and agree to fish it on alternate days. I secured Doug as my regular crew, and he fished with Buller as well. On Buller's days I would return to Balconie, which the other two Babes fished on the days I was absent.

The rent was on the steep side, but I reckoned that given an average season we could turn a reasonable profit. I was wrong. For a start, the first year was the wettest one I have known. May wasn't too bad – we had a couple of dozen big fish – but then it started to rain, and how. My diary records 'rain', 'rain', 'rivers in spate', 'the run is away to the rivers', 'gloom', 'anger', 'sickness', 'disappointing', 'they'd better come soon' (on 11 July), and then on 24 July, 'Thunder, rain, big spate'. The final indignity came on the last day of the season with 'One pox-ridden fish'. I remember it well. Doug and I were in the boat and we saw a strange-looking mark coming towards us, something swimming very high in the water with its dorsal fin occasionally breaking the surface. Nothing else was happening, we had to go for it, and it proved to be a smallish grilse absolutely covered in ulcers and scabs and evidently blind. We left it for the gulls.

The next year, my diary records on 10 May, 'The rivers are low for the first time since May last year.' The subsequent seasons were a little better, but I never made a fortune; in fact, we did very little better than break even. In retrospect, taking on the lease was a bad move. Prices had reached their peak and were being dragged down by

With Stan at Alness. (*ES*)

Doug and self. Weather vane at Blackhill Cottage. (*RR*)

the increasing numbers of farmed fish coming on to the market. I would have been better to stay content with Balconie, although those seasons were not great there, either.

When my lease came to an end, I didn't have to think long before surrendering it. Steve K took it on, and I went in briefly for another dubious venture (see the next chapter).

21

Nigg

Despite our scorn for 'banging' stations – where the netsmen just sweep continuously rather than spot fish – I did spend two seasons (just the month of July, to be strictly accurate) banging on the beach at Nigg.

Nigg was once a tiny coastal village scattered along the small road which leads to the foot of the North Sutor, but since the early 1970s it has been the site of a huge oil rig fabrication yard, and the original village has been all but obliterated. My mother spent many happy holidays there in her young day (the 1920s and early 1930s), and what follows is extracted from the memories she recorded in old age:

> Nigg was the most glorious place, with a golden beach and wonderful views up the firth to Ben Wyvis. We had a lovely time – impromptu dances, golf tournaments, rowing to Cromarty. We seemed to know everyone of all varieties and mixed easily at golf, etc. Mother never fussed about where we were or what we were doing. We climbed the Sutor and hung over the cliffs. Robert and Hector [her young brothers] rowed about the firth, and even when their empty boat was seen tied to a buoy near Invergordon, she never worried (they had actually been hoisted aboard HMS *Hood* for a visit!). We had a wonderful dance at the pier head, lit by car headlights, and a boatload came over from Cromarty to join us. Rowing

Nigg in the old days. A Victorian watercolour.

to Cromarty was especially impressive when the Fleet was in and dozens of warships lay at anchor, dominated by HMS *Hood*, which lay quite close to Nigg as she was too big to 'swing' further up the firth. Naval officers in flocks came to tea, including Admiral Jellicoe [Commander of the Grand Fleet at the battle of Jutland in 1916], who looked like a small tortoise. I was much embarrassed when he walked into the upstairs drawing room at Little Dunskaith [the house they stayed in, long since demolished] just as I was unpacking some pants!

We had someone to cook and help in the house, and it was always a member of the McLeod family, who became dear friends for the rest of our lives – 'Wee Jess', the eldest, sweet and gentle, fiery Nell, so good looking with prematurely white hair, pink cheeks and aquiline features, and Dolly, the youngest, with round, pale cat's eyes. When young, they all had that real black hair that you see in many Highlanders. Mrs McLeod was asthmatic, always smelled of herbal cigarettes and had a voice like a peacock. Grannie, who wore a mutch [a close-fitting cap] and shawl, had to translate everything from Gaelic and lived in her own thatched cottage. I think the cottages were all thatched in those days with 'bent' grass from the edge of the sea. I had an eye for one of Nell's many cousins, Donald McLeod, who had been away in the Gulf and Canada in the oil business and had a wicked twinkle in his eye. Young people used to gather in the evening at 'the warmest place in Nigg', behind some thick whins at the Pitcalzean gate.

The Dance on the Pier.

Drawing by my great-aunt, Aline Wells.

Mum often took us to Nigg for picnics when we were children. Our favoured spot was in the 'bents', the coarse seaside grass which grows in the dunes just above the high water mark, sharp on bare legs but tall enough to give shelter from the wind. It was on the beach below this, just to the east of the pier, that we fished.

We worked one boat and two nets. These were about 150 yards long, almost twice the length of the nets I was used to, and somewhat deeper, too. The mesh was 4½" as opposed to 3½", but they were still a hard pull. When one net came in it would be piled on to a stretcher, ready to be set on the boat as soon as the other net was out. We rowed the net out slowly with a hook in it – an inverted J-shape, if you like – and then pulled it in very, very slowly; if we saw fish move inside the hook or hit the net, then we would pull hard to close the net up and take it right in. To comply with the law, a sweep net must be kept moving at all times, but any netsman will tell you that there are ways to make it look as if you are pulling, when actually you are just letting the rope slip through your hands. We didn't flout the law obviously – the beach was too public for that – but with those big nets and hard pulls, we didn't want many blanks.

It worked – kind of. We caught close to a thousand fish each season, but I don't recall making a lot out of it (I was working on a share basis with the Estate). Of course, we had to employ a big crew, which included: Gary McCrossan, half-Highlander, half-Glaswegian, a long-time devotee of the fishing and later a welder who in between his tours of duty on oil rigs in Kazakhstan or off the west coast of Africa would often spend time at Kiltearn with Rik and me. He died in a helicopter crash in Orkney almost a decade ago. Jack Turtiainen (the mad Finn) had made sergeant in the Finnish army at twenty-one, but found it too tame and joined the French Foreign Legion. He carried a big knife on his belt, and later, when he was working in the grain dryer at Foulis, I made the mistake of approaching him from behind when he couldn't hear me coming for the noise of the dryer. I tapped him on the shoulder, and before I knew it, he had whipped round and had the point of the knife up against my stomach. Robbie, a cheeky young fellow with a winning smile and an infectious giggle, had the best throwing arm I have ever seen; if it looked like fish were in danger of swimming out of the net, we would put Robbie to chucking stones in their path to head them off (another illegal manoeuvre, I believe, though I cannot think why). Then there was gentle Tommy, an old acquaintance from Balconie, Colin from Evanton and several others whose names I have forgotten.

I had an old green VW minibus to transport fish and crew, but it was a bit far to travel to Nigg every day, especially for an early tide, so the crew often slept in an old six-berth caravan in the dunes. This vehicle was very nearly the death of Jan and me. At the beginning of the Nigg season we planned to tow it down there with the Land Rover, and we duly collected it from Geordie's workshop. It seemed like the caravan's hitch was not fitting very snugly over the Land Rover's tow ball, but we got it on, and Stan whipped the attachment with some wire for extra security. We took it easy on the road, and all went well until we hit the beginning of the Tomich straight. Then something caught my eye just over my right shoulder and I turned my head to see …

Woah! The caravan had broken free and was overtaking us! We could only watch, horrified, as it sailed serenely by in the right-hand lane. But it must have been our lucky day – there was no traffic behind or in front, and nothing coming in the opposite direction; the caravan continued on the road for fifty yards or so, then mounted the right hand verge and parked itself neatly and safely, parallel to the road. It all happened so fast that there wasn't even time to scream.

One relic still standing of the old village was the Nigg Ferry Hotel. This was a handy source of refreshment for the crew, sometimes too handy, in fact – there were ugly scenes on the beach a couple of times when drink brought out some latent hostility between Jack and Gary, and I had to step in and calm things down. But the hotel was handy for me, and I took a small and rather squalid room there very cheaply for the season. We discovered by trial and error the best time to fish. Essentially, this was on an incoming tide – not because that was when the fish were there, but because it proved impossible to hold the net once the ebb tide got a grip. A couple of chancers were fishing the Castlecraig bag-net station just outside the Sutor and they kept their boat at the pier. They didn't seem to be catching much. Whenever we asked Eddie, the gadgie in charge, he would say, 'Just heads and tails, head and tails! The seal had the best of them.' They sometimes gave us a hand, and at the first sign of the tide turning, Eddie would pipe up, 'It's the ebb, George boy, the ebb.' It was his theme song, and inevitably he became known to us as 'Eddie the Ebb'.

We caught a lot of fish which looked 'foreign' to me: short, chunky creatures, quite unlike the Cromarty Firth natives and probably heading for the Beauly or the Ness. We also caught plenty of sea trout, often big ones up to 6lbs. Then there were partans (edible crabs). These were a major nuisance in the net, but a welcome bonus once disentangled and put in the pot.

Nigg was an interesting interlude. I am glad to have experienced a banging station, but when the Estate surrendered their lease I didn't miss it. It couldn't compare with the joys of proper fishing.

22

Tide, Wind and Water

The biggest spring tides in the firth see a difference of getting on for five metres between low and high water. In the inner firth, the ebb of a big tide can look as if Neptune has pulled the plug and all the water has drained out. Even well to the east of the bridge – actually, it is more like a causeway – there is almost more dry land, in the shape of sandbanks, than there is water, and west of the bridge there is only a narrow channel. Gerald, a Dutch forester for the Estate and a friend of the fishing, could not understand why the decision was taken to build a bridge. If this was Holland, it would have been a dam. Above it, the land would be drained, with a channel for the Conon, and after ten years or so you would have thousands of acres of new farmland.

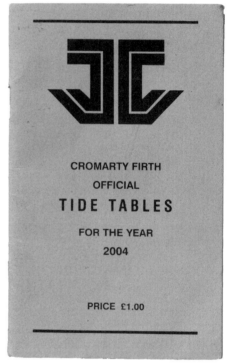

CROMARTY FIRTH
OFFICIAL
TIDE TABLES
FOR THE YEAR
2004

PRICE £1.00

Tide tables – the fisherman's bible.
(*John Lawrence-Jones*)

Once the firth was crossed by many ferries, between Nigg and Cromarty, at Invergordon, Alness and Foulis, but only the first of these has survived the building of fast roads and of the bridge itself. Our fishing, the year the bridge was being built, was accompanied by the thump, thump, thump of the piles being driven into the mud. Somewhere towards Dingwall there is also a point where carts once crossed at low water, but as children we were always warned not to venture out on to the ebb there, because there are quicksands.

The tide governs everything at the fishing. There are only a few places in the firth where you can sweep at high water – the beaches at Nigg, Alness, Balconie, Balachladdich ('shore town'), Foulis and Ardullie – and only at Alness and Balconie, close to rivers, can you regularly spot fish. Everywhere else it is too shallow at high water to work a net, so most of our fishing has been at low water, when the tide goes out enough to expose a cairn or bank close to deeper water. In practice, this means going out about three hours before low water and coming in up to three hours after it.

There are two tides every day, and the time of the tide advances every day, by about half an hour on spring tides and sometimes more than an hour on neaps. The tide is a mysterious phenomenon. Neap tides in the firth can sometimes behave very oddly, starting to ebb, then stopping, or occasionally even coming in a little, before going out again. On the very smallest tides, the difference between high and low water is barely a metre and a half; a fisherman six feet tall standing at the edge of the ebb at the bottom of low water would still have his head above the surface at the top of the flood. These small tides are always in the middle of the day and are rarely great for fishing. There are sometimes long and tedious hours on the cairn, when neither tide nor fish appears to move at all, and the only relief is a game of 'cairn killer' – a bit like conkers, you both pick a big stone and take turns trying to smash your opponent's with yours.

On these very neap tides with low water in the middle of the day you only get one fishing session, since the other, twelve hours later, falls during the hours of darkness.

Pensioners watching the water. Self and Steve K. (*JH*)

The bigger tides offer a morning and an evening, although in latter years we very rarely fished them both. The real monster tides – I have seen 0.0m on the chart, in other words the absolute bottom ever recorded – are always interesting. Starfish appear, as do sponges. You get to see the ground over which the net is pulled on smaller tides. Quite close to Kiltearn, rarely seen sandbanks emerge, great places for a swim if there isn't much doing, but also occasionally fishable – Steve K and I pulled a good shot one day on the bank off the Balachladdich beach. On these tides there is virtually no slack water: they drain fast and come in equally quickly, so there is a lot of movement from cairn to cairn to find fishable water.

I have often wondered which we catch more fish on, the ebb or the flood. I suspect it has been pretty even over the years, confirming our observation that fish move up and down the firth in a fairly random manner. Buller reckoned that there were two crucial moments – when the tide stopped ('the low water fish') and when it turned ('first of

'The last knockings'. The supermarket trolley, courtesy of Tesco, doing its job with the piece-bags. (*JH*)

Flat calm. (*JH*)

the flood') – and fish often seemed to appear just as we were about to be washed off the cairn ('the last knockings'). But the pattern is by no means fixed.

The other factor we always have to consider is the wind. East wind we generally like: in the summer months it is very rarely too strong and often accompanies good weather. West wind is fine, too, except that it is more likely to blow hard and stir up the mud near the edge; fish will not swim into dirty water. Summer gales always come from the south-west, and I can picture a typical one at the bothy – under a cloudless sky, big, stiff rollers pounding the beach, the boat long out of the water and the crew inside cooking up a stew. North wind is not good because it blows the fresh water, which is what the fish are following, straight out into the deep instead of along the shore. A touch of north in an east or west wind, however, can be good news, because it gives a lead-in to fish which might otherwise pass by out wide. South wind, although relatively rare, is not good to us; sure, it keeps the fresh in at the shore, but it makes spotting fish almost impossible, for instead of watching downwind you are looking across it, and the ripples on the surface all look like fish. Remember, of course, when I talk of wind direction, that we are fishing on the north shore of the firth and we treat it as if it runs west to east, whereas it is actually more like south-west to north-east.

Sometimes there is no wind, and that can be fine, especially in the early morning or in dull weather. It's not much good if it's bright, warm or sunny – then fish are disinclined to swim into shallower water, and all we can do is watch the heads cruise by out of reach in the deep. Spotting fish in a calm can be surprisingly difficult. Any little thing – a finnock's jump, a shoal of sprats, a pulsing jellyfish, a puff of wind – can leave a mark, and fish tend to swim deeper in calm water and can creep up on you unaware.

Shots on calm mornings are often last-minute scrambles, rather than the considered efforts of days when the spotting conditions are good and you get your first sight of fish a hundred yards away or more. On calm mornings it's not uncommon to be startled out of your reverie, spilling your tea and dropping your roll-up in the bilges, when a grilsie you never saw coming splashes a few feet from the boat. Even worse is a 'lumpy calm', when the surface is placid but there is a swell to the body of the water. This is so like the look of fish that it is extremely difficult to spot him in it.

The wind can be fluky, too. There are days when it goes all round the clock in the course of a single tide. This often happens when there's rain about. The turn of the tide frequently brings a change of wind, and a classic July morning on the firth will unfold as follows: at first light a gentle offshore breeze, which then dies; calm until low water; then, when the tide turns, a line shows in the water far away, to east or west, which is the day's wind advancing. Very occasionally, something extraordinary may happen: two different winds on the firth at the same time. One morning, we were fishing

A cold day on the cairn.

the Balconie bank in a light westerly and we could see a curious patch of rough water halfway across the bay to Alness. When we got back to the bothy, Doug appeared. He had been fishing at Alness, not much more than a mile away as the herring gull flies, and they had had an east wind all the tide. That patch of water we saw must have been where Doug's east wind and our westerly met.

Wind on the water and wind over land are two very different animals. There's more of it on the water, and it's a lot cooler. It's difficult to convince newcomers to the fishing to take enough clothes out with them. It's a lovely sunny day, they think, why would you need a sweater and a waterproof jacket? But as soon as you leave the land and start walking across the ebb to the cairns there's a perceptible drop in temperature; and when you have been standing out for an hour in the stiff easterly which often goes with sunny weather, a wind which has come to you across the North Sea, you will miss those extra layers. And when you come in from a tide, walking back up the shore, there is always a delicious moment when the warm air and the scents of the land strike senses which have been stripped clean by the hours of sea breezes.

Wind is one of the things which affects the appearance of what I have spent so many thousands of hours watching – the waters of the firth. Water-watching is one of the great joys of our fishing. I suppose there are times when it is less appealing – with a steady, chilly north-easterly wind, say, under low cloud, when sky and water are a uniform grey – but the firth has moments of beauty or interest on every other sort of day. Its natural colour is a gunmetal grey, but a fine day turns the water Mediterranean blue, and loveliest of all are the days when sun and cloud combine to create the shimmer of a molten precious metal on the surface. After a strong wind, there may be foam on the water, and this often settles into herringbone shapes, or spirals and whorls like some op art painting. Where we fish, the combination of fresh and salt means that the water is nearly always patterned, the fresh lying in calmer glossy streaks among the ripples of the salt. What we like to see are good big strips of fresh running along the shore to give himself a taste of the river and bring him towards us.

Then there's 'jabble', the fisherman's bane. Wind against tide, or a changeable wind, can create movement on the surface which is so like the mark of fish that seeing him in it is tricky. In extreme cases – as when an east wind is battling the tidal current ripping out of the Foulis bay – the sight becomes impossible. At other times you can still spot fish in it; there is something distinctive about the signs of actual life, and fish move, whereas jabble stays in the same place. Nevertheless, it is a frequent source of confusion and comment. 'What price are Bannerman's paying for jabble this year?' we used to enquire, when a mark proved not to be fish. And Doug and Old Paul between them coined this saying, oft-repeated: 'You can speculate ["Is that fish?"], you can gesticulate [pointing], you can even, prematurely, ejaculate ["Fish!"] – but if the fish no there, you no catch him!'

Sometimes the water looks so 'fishy' that you just know there is going to be action. Here's a typical case. We are on the inside cairn at Kiltearn, an evening low water with a steady south-easterly breeze. It's bright, but although we are looking west, there

Rough water. We are about to pack it in.

is enough cloud to screen what Buller would have called 'a dirty sun'. The water is a light grey colour, there is a touch of jabble outside us where the current has a grip, but otherwise the wavelets are producing a regular pattern, easy on the eye. Snaking down from the mouth of the Skiach behind us are glossy strips of fresh water, which combine to form a kind of pool a couple of hundred yards in front – not far, as it happens, from the site of the ancient fish trap. It's one of those tides when you get plenty of warning, and sure enough, on the edge of the gloss, an unmistakeable heave strikes up. 'Here's fish …'

As well as the salt or brackish water of the firth, we keep a good eye on the state of the rivers ('River up a touch. Let us pray …' records my diary one July day). If they run very dry then they may not be spilling enough fresh into the firth to attract fish in towards us. If they are in full spate, we can kiss the fishing goodbye for a few days, for all the fish in the firth will run them. Something in between is ideal: enough water to deliver good strips of fresh and draw fish in with the promise of a run, but not enough to provoke them all into a headlong dash inland. A big spate is quite a sight. The normal chatter over the stones of a small Highland river like the Alness, Black Rock or Skiach at first grows louder, until it becomes a roar. But then, in a really big spate, the flow rises so high above the rocks of the river bed that it goes quiet – just walls of peaty water rushing silently to the sea. Seen from the hill above, a spate like that stains the

Dirty weather. (*DM*)

firth in a great fan around every river mouth. The most dramatic sight like this I ever saw came in the winter of 1985, when a huge spate caused a landslide into the Black Rock river above the gorge, shearing a whole hillside away and filling the river in with several million tons of gravel and sand, turning the firth brown.

If we do go out when there has been a spate, we sometimes see fish behaving as if they were in fresh water; when they come up, instead of the usual travelling sea-leap they perform a 'head and tail' rise, a manoeuvre which all river anglers will recognize.

Water-watching may be a form of meditation, but it has its own rules. First, look far away – a good head can show up hundreds of yards off, and a jump even further – then scan to left and right. Then check out the water nearer to the boat; fish often pop up very close, perhaps coming in out of the deep and turning, and then you have to be quick: shout to the crew, up with the anchor, grab the oars, and all the while watch to see where he's going. Of course, there are tides, increasingly frequent in recent years, when watching empty water is all we do. But because you never know when or where fish may appear, you have to keep watching.

And if you are not watching the water, there is always the sky. Some days are blue, others are grey, but I have seen most colours above the firth over the years. Black or indigo when a storm is brewing; cream to apricot to peach as a morning dawns; pink to brick red to blazing scarlet as the sun sets over the monument on Cnoc Fyrish; even a strange green one evening, in the aftermath of a thunder storm. Because the views are long, twenty miles to the east and nearer fifty away to the hills in the west, there is a

Jonathan and rainbow.

lot of sky; and because we are in the eastern Highlands, with hills and sea around us, there is a lot of weather, often several different days in the sky at the same time. The annual rainfall at the furthest west point we can see is double that of the furthest point to the east. No two days on the water are the same.

23

The River with Three Names

The Black Rock, the Allt Graad ('ugly burn'), the Glass ('grey/green') – three names for the same water, a small Highland spate river which runs just half a dozen miles from its source in long, deep Loch Glass down to the firth. Not that fish can reach the loch, for just a couple of miles inland the river emerges in a fall from the Black Rock Gorge, which no salmon can run. Surrounded by the grand trees and lush undergrowth of Evanton Wood, a mile long and over a hundred feet deep but narrow enough to be crossed in places by a daring jump, this cleft in the sandstone is a natural wonder. From the two footbridges which span it, summer tourists gaze down at the water in the depths, but a really big winter spate will bring the river boiling halfway up the chasm. Naturally, there is a legend associated with the place: the Lady of Balconie, after whom our boat is named, is said to have been lured into the gorge by the devil, and her cries for help can still be heard issuing from its mouth.

Downstream of the gorge, the river flows through the village of Evanton and thence to the firth. The final few hundred yards, below the ford which we used to get to the Balconie bothy, were straightened and embanked, presumably during the era of eighteenth- or early nineteenth-century agricultural 'improvement', to drain and reclaim the low-lying fields of Balconie. The Skiach, the other river of Balconie, which flows down from Ben Wyvis has had the same treatment, and I often try to imagine what the place must have been like before this happened, when the two rivers would have met in acres of marsh and salt marsh, an absolute paradise for birds.

The river, by whatever name, is what makes Balconie Point such a fine fishing station. The Point's clean, pebbly beach jutting out into the firth is a natural landfall for fish coming in from the sea; but the water of the Black Rock streaming away to the east, supplemented by the Skiach just a few hundred yards to its west, is what calls them in.

We often fished low water at the mouth of the Black Rock. There were no artificial cairns here; instead, we worked from a shifting series of musselbanks. These could be treacherous underfoot – glutinous, smelly black mud which threatened to pull your waders off – but usually the mussels themselves formed a crust which was safe to walk on, and over time sand and gravel would build up too. Every year their formation would look slightly different, and in the final Balconie years a new one appeared, on its own and well out from the river mouth. We had a lot of fish there, although it was extremely sticky to stand on. I recall a morning tide there with Doug and his female

Doug's girls: Fiona and Gillian. (*FC*)

crew – lots of big shots and rowing home happy, all of us covered in mud and the girls' pretty faces spattered with black.

Because of the configuration of the banks and the shallow water in close, you had to fish clever here. A typical shot would go something like this. The wind is in the west, and I spot fish a long way off when they swim across a small bank which is just underwater. Then he disappears. Cut out? Turned back? It's impossible to say. No, he has just gone into a deep pot between banks, and up he pops again, closer to us now but further out.

I call to the bank, 'I'm going to get out a bit. Give us plenty rope.'

I'm on the bow oars, and Stevie is in the stern. Eddie is on the bank. We row out a few strokes, and I stand up at the oars for a better look, but there's no sign of him. The bottom in front of us is very uneven, and fish can easily be turned when they hit a shallow patch.

I fear he may be keeping out wide so I shout to Eddie, 'Pull a wee bit!' and fifteen feet of net come off into the water. It's as well to be prepared, in case he shows up again, and it's no sweat to re-pile a bit of net if the shot doesn't materialize.

Still no sign of him, but then a shout from Ed: 'He's in close here!'

Sure enough, he is showing again, tight in to the musselbank which curves out in front of us, and about thirty yards away.

'OK, but I'm not getting his head.' All I can see is a heave in the shallows. He could be going anywhere.

Then he begins to show again. 'He's heading out! Pull away. We'll go down and cut him off.'

Stevie and I row a big wide shot, and not long after we turn for home we run out of net.

'I'm coming past you, Stevie', I say and I drop my oars, hop over the stern thwart and on to the backboard, then grab the boat rope and jump into the water.

An aborted shot. Fish have disappeared when the net is half off, and we are re-piling it.

It's not really too deep for this manoeuvre, but unfortunately I am wearing my skipper's Bulldog waders which are a little short of full thigh length, and so, as we say, I 'get the bag wet'. Never mind, it's a fine day and not cold. I pass some rope behind my back, get a good grip on it and start walking the net back in, occasionally stopping to flack the rope on the water and scare fish away from the gap.

For once the coil of rope at Stevie's feet does not tangle as he rows back to the bank, and pretty soon he has the boat anchored and is adding his weight to the pull. The water near the bank is very shallow, which is handy for a shot like this – he is not likely to swim right in and get out under a rope – but it means that the end of the pull is tricky. It's obvious when the bag is still fifteen yards from the shore that the fish are in it – you can see them splashing – but it's so shallow there's a danger the net will roll round the ground rope. We take it carefully, however; the net keeps its shape, the bag is good and we drag seven fish through the mud and on to the mussels.

It's not a great haul, but there is much satisfaction in a difficult shot executed to perfection.

A tricky-looking shot. The net is well out, and if we are not careful, it will close up on itself. (*DM*)

24

Fish in Trouble

There is no doubt that Atlantic salmon are in trouble. In 2019 the chief executive of Fisheries Management Scotland declared, 'This iconic species is now approaching crisis point', and I cannot argue with that. The following numbers can only be a best estimate, but it is thought that in the heyday of my fishing life, the mid-1960s to the late 1980s, somewhere between one and two million fish were returning to Scotland's rivers from the sea every year. Now it is probably fewer than a third of that number. In the same years, the global population – for remember, our fish swims up the rivers of almost all the lands around the North Atlantic – has decreased by about the same amount. And it's not just himself that's in trouble. A study published in 2020 and led by the Zoological Society of London concluded that populations of migratory river fish of all species worldwide have seen a 'catastrophic' fall of 76 per cent since 1970.

Now some more figures. In 1967, the peak year since reliable statistics have been available, the year of 3,000 fish at Balconie, when Buller bought a car with his share, the total Scottish catch (nets and rods) was just over 600,000 fish; more than 250,000 were caught by net and coble fishermen, the fixed nets took slightly fewer, and the rods about 80,000. Now consider 2019 (I am ignoring 2020, because of the pandemic a completely atypical year). The total catch was 47,515, virtually all caught on rod and line and over 90 per cent of which were then released. The fixed nets, of course, had already gone; the haaf nets on the Solway, a local method peculiar to the area, took 164 fish; and the *total* catch for the whole season by Scotland's few surviving net and coble men was just 465 fish – fewer than we sometimes had, back in the day, in a single week at Balconie or Alness. And to bring it home, at Kiltearn in 2000–05 we averaged round eighty fish a season; in 2013–18 the average catch was just thirteen.

So what has gone wrong? A great deal of effort has gone into answering this question, but there is still no definitive explanation. What we can say is that Scotland's rivers are still producing decent numbers of smolts, but fewer than five in every hundred now return as adult fish, a drop of some 70 per cent in just the last twenty-five years. In other words, the problem seems to lie out at sea. It appears that any given river has a relatively fixed number of smolts it is able to produce; this depends on the availability of suitable spawning sites and perhaps levels of predation and quantities of food for fry and parr; popular spawning sites may be used by later-running fish, who 'overcut' the redds used by earlier fish and so destroy their eggs. There is thus no direct relationship between the number of spawning adults and of subsequent smolts, until the population of adults falls below a certain threshold; and given the thousands of eggs which a hen salmon produces, that population may be relatively low and still produce sufficient eventual smolts.

Scientific research has identified a number of other issues of concern. It has been suggested that fish are reaching the smolt stage earlier and leaving the river when they are smaller, thus reducing their chances of survival at sea. This may be a consequence of climate change. There also appears to have been a big reduction recently in the number of fish returning more than once to spawn – again suggesting that there are problems at sea.

What can be done? Stocking of rivers with parr or smolts may have some effect, but it is counter-productive unless fish native to the river are used, since every river has a genetically distinct stock of fish, adapted to the specific conditions of their own water and to their migration routes at sea. Artificially reared smolts, however, even if from eggs in their native river, do not return in big numbers, apparently lacking the skills required to avoid predators or catch prey. And in any case, if the problems lie out at sea, there is a high chance that these stocked fish will never return. Commercial netting of salmon is now effectively dead, and more than 90 per cent of the fish caught by anglers are put back, so human predation has mostly been brought to an end.

A great deal of effort is now being put into research aimed at increasing our understanding of smolts' behaviour. The Atlantic Salmon Trust's 'Missing Salmon Project' (atlanticsalmontrust.org/themissingsalmonproject/), which was launched in 2019, is Europe's largest programme of tagging and tracking smolts. They are tagged in the rivers around the Moray Firth, the area through which a fifth of all the UK's smolts pass, and their movements are then tracked in the rivers, the estuaries and the outer Moray Firth. The programme includes the Conon, the chief river of the Cromarty Firth. It is early days for the project, but one very surprising finding has already emerged: about half of the smolts tagged in the first year went missing *before* they reached salt water, suggesting that the problems do not all lie at sea – although the effect of tagging on a smolt's life expectancy cannot be discounted.

The eventual aim of the Missing Salmon Project (a similar study has now started on the west coast), which now involves a range of angling and conservation bodies in what is known as the Missing Salmon Alliance, is to understand why so many of our fish are missing, and to this end the project has constructed what it calls the 'Likely Suspects Framework', in other words the factors which contribute to salmon mortality. These are:

- Forestry and agriculture
- Avian predation
- Estuarine predation
- Coastal nets and aquaculture
- Marine predation
- Marine exploitation
- Climate change

Forestry and agriculture

This refers to things like the run-off of agricultural chemicals; afforestation of hillsides which leads to the acidification of spawning burns and consequent thickening of the shells of salmon eggs, damaging their ability to hatch; or forestry ploughing, which causes hillsides to drain quickly and thus river levels to rise and fall unnaturally fast. A particular issue on many rivers is the loss of bankside vegetation through over-grazing by sheep and deer (numbers of both are believed by most people to be far too high in Scotland). This causes all sorts of problems, from increased erosion of river banks and elevated summer water temperatures to a shortage in the water of the invertebrates on which fry and parr feed. Like the removal of weirs or other obstructions to migrating fish, these are things completely within man's control and can be tackled, providing the political will is there.

Avian predation

I suspect that the two biggest avian predators on young fish in the river are cormorants and saw-billed ducks (mergansers and goosanders); cormorants may also take smolts in the estuary. Fishermen have traditionally detested them all, and at one time fishery boards placed a bounty on their heads; Buller used to make some handy money in the winters shooting cormorants for the Conon board. Nowadays, all three can be shot under licence, but such licences are only likely to be issued to trout farms and the like. The culling of any species raises tricky ethical and ecological issues, but there is no doubt that these birds take a good many fry, parr and smolts, and the populations of the saw-bills are concentrated in Scotland.

Estuarine predation

Every spring or early summer, the newspapers carry photographs taken from Chanonry Point or Fort George, at the narrows in the inner Moray Firth. They show a dolphin tossing a salmon in the air. People love dolphins, of course, and Chanonry Point is a popular tourist viewing spot, but the bottlenose dolphin population of around hundred individuals which use the Moray Firth as their base are serious predators on salmon. Fish returning to the Ness and the Beauly must all pass through the narrows at Chanonry Point, scarcely half a mile wide, and the dolphins know it.

These dolphins are relatively recent arrivals in the area. When I started fishing, there were none here; porpoises were what we regularly saw – also predators on salmon, of course, but less effective hunters than the dolphins, although the latter only occasionally enter the Cromarty Firth. The salmon's traditional enemy in the water is the seal. In the outer firths these are likely to be grey seals. A hundred years ago, when they were regularly hunted, the UK population is estimated to have fallen as low as 500 individuals; now it is over 100,000, and a mature grey seal will eat up to 11kg

'Henry' – a common seal.

of fish a day. Fishermen and fish farmers can obtain a licence to shoot seals which are bothering their nets, but this can be problematic. Tourists love watching seals, and people find the idea of killing the big-eyed creatures abhorrent. Accidents can happen, too. Not long ago, some bag-net fishermen of our acquaintance were going out to lift their net off the Easter Ross coast and spotted a sleek black head coming out of the water near the bag. The skipper reached for his rifle, drew a bead on it … and then it turned round. It was a diver in a wetsuit who escaped death by a fraction of a second.

What we see inside the firth are nearly all common (harbour) seals, smaller than their grey cousins. There are about 30,000 of them in the UK and they tend to hug the coast, unlike the greys which travel far to feed and breed. In the past I have counted well over a hundred hauled out on the sandbanks close to the Cromarty Firth bridge, but it seems that their numbers are currently declining locally.

Studies of seals' feeding habits in the firths have suggested that salmon are not a major part of their diet. However, salmon are not available in any quantity except at certain times of year, and there is no question but that seals will then hunt them. They used to plague the bag-net stations, and we have often seen Henry with his head out of the water and a fish in his jaws.

Coastal nets and aquaculture

The nets can be discounted; they have virtually disappeared. Aquaculture, i.e. salmon farming, is a different matter, and when people ask me what I think about it, I tend to reply, 'Don't get me started' or 'How long have you got?'

It began in Norway in the 1960s and has become a staple Scottish industry, employing at least 1,500 people. Very few West Highland sea lochs or island bays are not now disfigured by a 'group' or two of salmon cages. Quite apart from the visual pollution, and the distasteful nature of any form of factory farming (for that is what it is, thousands of fish densely packed into a relatively small space), the farms are magnets for disease and parasites; the sea trout population of the West Highlands, fish which spend their lives in these coastal waters, has been decimated by the effect of sea lice spreading from the farms. These parasites attack the head and neck of fish, and can literally eat them alive. The sea bed underneath the cages becomes a wasteland of rotting food and fish faeces. Research has shown that the presence of salmon farms near a river leads to an average 30 per cent drop in numbers of returning wild fish.

The salmon farming industry has a lamentable record when it comes to addressing these issues; their own so-called Code of Good Practice is far from strict or universally obeyed, and they have resisted suggestions for reform, such as the relocation of farms away from the migration routes of wild fish. Now the industry is seeking permission to use a neonicotinoid insecticide to control sea lice on their fish. Neonicotinoids were banned from agricultural use by the EU in 2018 because they were killing bees; they are 7,000 times as toxic as DDT, and soluble in water. In the 1990s the eel and smelt fisheries of Lake Shinji in Japan collapsed after neonicotinoids used on surrounding farmland leached into the water, killing the invertebrates on which the fish fed. A recent leading article in *British Wildlife* magazine calls for a ban on their use in fish farming, because 'we risk discovering in twenty or thirty years' time that the marine environment near salmon farms is chronically contaminated with a potent and indiscriminate neurotoxin, with who-knows-what consequences for marine life and fisheries.'

A single big farm may hold more fish than the entire world population of wild Atlantic salmon, and the worst thing from the wild salmon's point of view is that so many fish escape from the farms. For at least the last ten years, the catch returns which every fishery has to submit to the Scottish government have contained a column, alongside 'salmon', 'grilse' and 'sea trout', for 'farmed escapes'. In 2018 there were three large escapes in Scotland: 22,000 from Skye, 48,000 from Colonsay and 74,000 from the Western Isles. In August 2020, 50,000 escaped on the Argyll coast, and a further 36,000 died. And fish escape from Norwegian farms, too – 140,000 in 2018 and almost 300,000 in 2019. Many of these will not survive long; they have been bred to be fat and docile, precisely what you do not want to be as a wild fish, and the first shark, seal or orca they meet will have them. But unfortunately some do survive, meet up with wild fish, follow them into their river and breed with them. This amounts to 'genetic pollution', since every river system has a genetically distinct population of fish, their size, form, age of smolting and shape of eggs all adapted to it. And will the offspring of a farmed fish ever find its way back to its native river?

Moreover, Atlantic salmon are now being farmed in places far from their home – in Chile and Tasmania and on the Pacific coast of North America – and here, too, they escape. In August 2020 some 100,000 escaped from a Chilean farm after their cages were wrecked by a storm, and more than 700,000 died after sixteen of the cages sank to the sea bed. Goodness knows what the live escapees and the rotting remains of the dead will have done to the local environment.

So can you eat farmed salmon with a clear conscience? Personally, I never do, unless it would be unbearably rude to a host or hostess not to, and I discourage others from buying it. But there is a solution: do not farm salmon in cages in the open sea, do it in tanks on land into which you pump sea water and from which you can dispose of the waste safely. Fish bred like this might be more expensive, of course, but the industry would no longer be polluting Scotland's coastal waters or devastating the wild stock.

Marine predation

This is difficult to estimate, or to do anything about. Post-smolts at sea may be prey for a variety of species, while grown salmon in the sea are probably taken by a range of larger predators, from tuna to sharks to toothed whales.

Marine exploitation

Now that the Greenland and Faroes fisheries have closed, there is no substantial high-seas fishery which targets salmon specifically. And since wild salmon, in the UK at least, have disappeared from dinner tables, there is little incentive for illegal fishing. They may, however, be caught as 'by-catch' by boats fishing for other species or trawling generally. In the nature of things, there is little information on this.

Climate change

This is the big imponderable. Not whether it is happening – we know it is – but what effect it is having on our fish. Warmer water in rivers may encourage earlier smolting and thus cause fish to leave the river when smaller and less well able to look after themselves. More violent storms, another consequence of global heating, also mean more cages wrecked and bigger escapes from salmon farms. Warmer seas have already affected some fish populations – bass and bluefin tuna moving further north, cod declining in the North Sea – and it is strongly suggested that the species which provide crucial food for salmon at sea may also be moving.

In the last decade or so, it is well known that the populations of northern seabirds which rely for food on krill, sand eels and other small fish – terns, puffins, kittiwakes, guillemots – have been in trouble. This may reflect increased predation of small fish by swelling populations of herring and mackerel which have moved north as water temperatures have warmed in the North Atlantic. And the food which the mackerel and herrings are gobbling up is precisely that which post-smolts and growing grilse rely on.

Of course, it is within humanity's power to slow down, halt or even reverse manmade global heating – but your guess is as good as mine if we will ever achieve it.

* * *

It is easy to become gloomy about the Atlantic salmon's prospects. But it's not all bad news. For a start, there are now a number of organizations, local, national and international, devoted to the conservation of salmon: to research into their lives, publicizing their plight and putting pressure on governments to take action. The Atlantic Salmon Trust (AST), which operates the Moray Firth smolt-tracking project, does much excellent work; the North Atlantic Salmon Conservation Organisation (NASCO) is currently undertaking a three-year research programme; and in a global initiative to raise public awareness, 2019 was designated International Year of the Salmon.

While it is difficult to improve the salmon's chances at sea, the rivers are a different matter. In pre-industrial times most northern and north-western European rivers of any size will have had a run of salmon. The Thames certainly did, and the Rhine was once famous for its very big fish. The Thames Salmon Trust, founded in the 1980s, has made heroic efforts to restore salmon to the river, but so far without great success. However, the opening of the Thames Tideway Tunnel, the so-called super-sewer, due

A beauty – note the sea lice on the tail.

to become operational in 2024, will make the river in London even cleaner than it already is. I live in hope that one day I will spot a jumper on my morning walk between Putney and Hammersmith bridges. And some salmon rivers have already been restored to health: fish now run the Tyne and the Clyde, for example, once filthy rivers which had not seen them for a century or more.

The rod-fishing statistics offer another chink of light. Scotland's rod fishermen may have had poor sport in the last couple of years – 2018's catch was the lowest on record, and 2019 the fourth lowest – but these were very dry years, not good for river fishing; the early years of the twenty-first century saw good numbers caught, and 2010's was the highest catch since 1952.

Salmon runs have always been liable to cyclical fluctuation, for reasons which are not always apparent. The big grilse runs of the 1960s and 70s, for example, may have been due to elevated levels of plankton and consequently rich feeding in the North Atlantic. Spring-running fish, which were dominant in the mid-twentieth century, declined later. In the late nineteenth century, grilse were dominant, as they were in the later twentieth; large autumn fish were also a feature of the later 1800s, as they have been again in some recent years. In the 1880s and the 1950s–70s catches were much higher than in the 1910s, 1940s or 1980s and 90s. So who is to say that, for reasons we do not fully understand, big runs of silver may not return to Scotland's firths and rivers? Whether there will be any netsmen to catch them, however, is a different matter.

25

The Salmon in the Glass Case

Christopher ('Tif') Eccles

In a glass case above the mantelpiece,
A stuffed salmon, grey, wax-wrinkled,
Parched in an airless void. Is this all that remains
Of that bright quivering arrow of silver?

Now the sea is full of metal cages
Brimming over with lost souls.
A shining, pulsing fish, as long as your arm,
Which once swam as far as the Greenland sea,

Now loses its mind in a salmon farm cage.
Hundreds are heaped together, nourished with pellets
Made from the sweepings of the abattoirs.
Here is our modernity, a zone of cruelty,

A concentration camp for the supermarket shelf.
We make an industry from nature and call it progress,
We take beauty and hatch and herd it blind
Into these sterile aquariums of hopelessness.

Tif, a friend of Rod's, was an occasional visitor to the fishing and is clearly a man with his heart in the right place.

26

Rods versus Nets

Salmon anglers have always had it in for netsmen. My dentist, a keen rod fisherman, used to greet me by saying, only half in jest, 'Ah, here comes the salmon killer!' and would proceed, once he had me at his mercy in the chair, unable to respond and with my mouth full of hardware, to harangue me about the evils of netting. There's nothing new about this antagonism. In 1828, Sir Humphry Davy, the great chemist and inventor, complained:

> The commercial netsmen on the Tweed are taking all the salmon out of the river and it is terrible. The only chance of fishing the fly is on Sundays when the nets are not working.

Back in 1962, the Hunter Committee, charged with making recommendations about the legislation governing salmon fisheries, stated:

> A salmon caught or available for catching by rod and line generally contributes more to the Scottish economy than a salmon caught for commercial purposes, and as the commercial fishing effort is applied before the fish reach the main angling areas, the commercial catch should be so regulated as to allow attractive and reasonably successful angling.

I cannot argue with that. Hotels, tackle shops, fishing rentals, ghillies' jobs – all these and more depend on anglers wanting to catch Scotland's 'king of fish'. For the last thirty years or so the rod fishermen have caught more fish than the netsmen, and now that netting has almost disappeared, they account for virtually the whole catch. You might therefore think that the age-old antagonism of the rod men for the netsman would simply have disappeared; in effect, the rods have won the day, especially now that they can point to their virtuous practice of returning to the water nearly every fish they catch.

However, I believe that it is still worthwhile looking at the past uneasy relationship between rods and nets. It is an argument I have entered into myself at times, occasionally in letters to the angling press, more often in conversation with rod fishermen. A letter of mine in the *Economist* in 2015, in response to an article by Orri Vigfússon, the godfather of salmon conservation, read as follows:

Orri Vigfússon calls for a halt to the 'killing of wild Atlantic salmon by any method' for three years in order to help salmon stocks recover. He is particularly critical of mixed-stock coastal netting. How does he account for the fact that until the late 1980s salmon were routinely killed by anglers, and coastal nets took far more fish than the tiny number they take today, yet stocks remained healthy? There must surely be plenty of other reasons for the Atlantic salmon's decline. Take your pick from salmon farming, booming seal populations, climate change, pollution, the poor management of rivers and illegal fishing on the high seas.

I write as one of those netsmen whom Mr Vigfússon wishes to put out of business.

The coastal nets have now almost all gone; I am indeed 'out of business'; and anglers kill very few of the fish they catch. Would I still write the same letter today? I'm not sure. But what is certain is that it is very hard to prove that there is, as many rod fishermen assert, a direct relationship between netting and falling numbers of fish. Reliable Scottish catch figures are available for every year since 1952, during which time the nets' catches have gone up, then down and are now effectively zero. And what has happened to the rods' catch in that time? Did it increase when the Atlantic Salmon Trust began to buy up and close down so many stations in the late 1980s and the Greenland and Faroese fisheries went shortly afterwards, or when all Scotland's bag nets were outlawed and the Northumberland drift-netters disappeared? No. The rod catch was actually lower in 1952 than in any year until the most recent couple. It has gone up and down in these seventy-odd years, but the peaks and troughs, which are not great, show no obvious correlation with the netting effort.

I would suggest, therefore, as my letter to the *Economist* indicated, that the reason for the salmon's decline is not over-fishing by the nets. I believe that most of Scotland's rivers once held, and many may still hold, a harvestable surplus of fish. Neil Graesser, a distinguished writer on angling matters, had this to say:

If it was left to natural predation, disease and angling to control the population of the species, there is little doubt that the spawning and feeding areas of the river system would in a very short space of time become grossly over-crowded probably with disastrous results. That is why a well controlled legitimate net fishery becomes an integral and essential part of fisheries management.

As I said earlier, there is no direct relation between the number of spawning adults and subsequent smolts, until the population of adults falls below a certain threshold. A relatively small number of spawners can produce enough eggs to sustain a river's population and provide sport for rods and a living for netsmen – provided that the smolts these eggs grow into return in sufficient numbers.

This is not to say, of course, since the fish definitely are in crisis and the symptom of this is the crash in smolt survival, that killing of salmon by any means, as Vigfússon

Older fishermen. Oz and I take it easy on the cairn, with Kiltearn kirk behind us. (*JH*)

proposed, should not be suspended. But it would be a sorry day if this meant that salmon netting had gone for good. John Bennett, in an appendix to his amusing novel *The Summer Crew* (Spey Publishing, 2020), puts it like this:

> The demise of the onshore salmon fisheries asks much bigger questions about how we manage our natural resources, protect our communities and preserve our natural heritage and identity. It is, of course, vital that we conserve our wildlife, but how do we also protect our communities and their traditions?

Alistair Stenhouse in his MSc dissertation of 2014 (*The Archaeology of Coastal Salmon Fishing in Easter Ross, an industry in terminal decline*) concluded:

> Unless salmon stocks in the North Atlantic make a demonstrated recovery, and there is agreement that wild salmon is a food resource and not only a means of

recreation, then the future of the coastal netting industry is one where the cobles, nets, other equipment and photographs of the fishers themselves will soon exist only in local heritage centres … The loss of employment and finance generated by salmon fishing has been indisputably important to the local communities, however of greater cultural concern is the loss of the unique technology, terminology and many place names, used by generations of salmon fishers to describe the landscape of Easter Ross. The technology may be recorded and displayed in heritage centres or in historical websites, however … it is likely that these names, this intimate knowledge of the landscape and the unique way of life associated with coastal salmon fishing may be soon lost forever.

In the case of our fishing, it is probably too late already. Virtually all of those who possess the crucial skill of spotting fish are now in their sixties or seventies, and there is no likelihood of their being able to pass the skill on to a younger generation. So it will die, and fishing 'on the long rope' as it was once known will be gone for good.

I will leave the last word on nets and rods to Iain Robertson, whose great study of coastal salmon fisheries (*The Salmon Fishers*, Medlar, 2013) ends like this:

Notwithstanding the concomitant accounts of human rivalries, stubbornness and stupidity, it should be recognized that supplying food is fundamental to human existence and netting wild salmon is a calling not without merit. There would appear to be little merit in debarring people the privilege of eating wild salmon merely because, at a particular juncture, a well-financed interest group demands the exclusive right to catch the Atlantic salmon for purely recreational purposes.

27

A Photographer at the Fishing

Over the years, a fair few visitors to the fishing, taken by the appeal of the place and the activity, have recorded our doings. We have had poets (Andrew McNeillie, George Huntley, Rik Parke, Tif Eccles) and artists (Robert Blake, Fionna Chalmers, Ingebjorg Smith). No musicians that I know of, although the haunting voice of Capercaillie's Karen Matheson on 'Fisherman's Dream' captures the nostalgia I feel for fishing days past.

We have been filmed on occasion. Finnian caught the action with his video camera back in the 1990s, and he also filmed a roe deer swimming across the firth. I have twice seen them do this, and they make short work of it, even with a fair tide running. Curious as to why a roe might do such a thing, I quizzed a stalker friend. 'Were they

Women on the cairn. (L to R) Pat, Romay, self, Rod. (*JH*)

Steve K. (*ES*)

young bucks?' he asked. Indeed they were, and he then said that they were almost certainly escaping from older bucks who were bullying them.

The unintentionally hilarious work of some professional filmmakers can still be seen in the Storehouse exhibition at Foulis Ferry. On their first site visit – a sunny day, with a couple of girls on the cairn – it was decided that something more authentic was required. I was firmly told that I was not ethnic enough, women were banned, and Doug and Steve K (neither of them local, the one from Fraserburgh and the other a Londoner) were cast as the stars. The resulting video I have always thought of as 'ZZ Top at the Fishing': one pony-tailed and bearded geezer rows the shot, while the other pulls the rope. When the net comes in it contains just the one fish, palpably dead already. Of course, no fish had appeared while the film crew were there, so they had to introduce one caught earlier that morning and already suffering from rigor mortis.

Lots of people have taken photographs of the fishing. The best amateurs have been Rod Richard, Dave McLachlan and Jonathan Harding, many of whose photographs appear in this book. But not long ago we were privileged to have a genuine professional on the cairn. John Lawrence-Jones, formerly stills photographer to *Spitting Image* and creator of many striking images for advertising and for magazines like *Country Life*, was putting together a series of pictures of great British foods and asked me if he could come and photograph some fish. Catches had already slumped at this date, and I warned John that it might be a wasted trip. However, he was going to be in Scotland anyway, to photograph shellfish on the west coast, he loves the Highlands, is a keen

Brenda poses on the east wind bench for Dave McLachlan. (*RR*)

rod fisherman and had been to the fishing with us back in the glory days – so he was determined to come.

The first few days bore out my worst expectations. The boat was leaking badly, and we had to take her out of the water for some emergency caulking; it was wet and cold; and we had no fish. However, the last morning of John's week did look a little more promising – a biggish tide and a steady easterly breeze, just right to get fish coming out of the Foulis bay. And for once, everything went right. The crew that day was just Rod and I, so we made John work and we had four shots, no blanks, nine fish. And what fish! Six were standard grilsies, but three were donkeys, 10lbs and upward and some of the most gorgeous creatures you ever saw. If I had ordered up models from a top agency, they couldn't have been more beautiful – sleekly silver and perfectly formed. We took the greatest care not to knock off a single one of their lovely scales.

John was pleased, although I don't think he quite realized how lucky he had been. Now came the business of taking their picture, and I offered to act as John's assistant. The first task was to find a suitable background, and his eye lit on the hessian sacks which we used to carry fish up the beach. These sacks, which I get from a London friend Trevor, who is in the business, originally held coffee beans and are ideal for the job. They can be soaked in the sea to keep fish moist and fresh, and they hide the catch from curious eyes – fishers never reveal, except to their intimates, exactly how many they have caught; 'Aye, we're getting one or two' can mean anything from one or two to a hundred. A sack will take at least half a dozen grilse, which two men can carry

Rod and self. (*JH*)

Two thumpers. (*John Lawrence-Jones*)

easily between them; the trick, taught us by Old Paul, is to twist each corner round a small pebble in order to create a convenient handhold.

John decided to photograph the fish from above, so we spread the sack on a fish box and laid the two best fish on it. John fiddled with them until he got them just the way he wanted, then positioned his camera (film, not digital) above. While I stood by with a cup of water to keep the fish moist and shiny, John nipped up and down his step ladder, checking the angles and taking some Polaroids through the lens of his camera. I was astonished that Polaroid cameras were still being used. The whole exercise took a good hour, but finally John had his picture, and it is superb. My copy is on the bookshelf beside me as I write, with my own caption:

Two thumpers from the Cromarty Firth – 10lbs and 12lbs
Kiltearn, July 2014

28

At Kiltearn

Another story here. It was never such a good station – no high-tide fishing, the deep water is further away so many fish pass out of reach, it's awkwardly shallow on big tides, and the little River Skiach doesn't spill a lot of fresh water into the firth or support much of a run of fish.

Of course, there were sometimes big shots here, good days, good weeks, even good seasons. And it was a place for big fish early on – I can see in my mind's eye Dave J triumphantly holding up a 22-pounder on the Foulis cairn in the first week of June.

But mostly the story of Kiltearn is a long coda to the history of the spotting stations. When Balconie, Alness and the Crown fishings all closed at the end of the 1980s, the

Munro country. Looking up to Ben Wyvis from the Kiltearn cairns. (*JH*)

Kiltearn kirk from the south-east. (*FC*)

only stations to remain active were on the stretch of shore where the rights belong to Munro of Foulis. For a year or two the Crown fishermen worked the edge of the ebb at Foulis Ferry near the girnel, the storehouse which once held the produce of Foulis estate before it was shipped out from the beach in front. They caught a few fish there – it's probably the furthest up the firth that they are reliably spottable – but it's a tricky place, lots of weed and pretty shallow. In the old days, when fish were still plentiful, I fished a tide there once with Oz and Rainbow in the stoners' coble, the *Mary Jane*. We had a shot – the only one of its kind I ever saw – with mullet, a sea trout and a flounder in it, as well as himself.

Later on, Rik and I fished a few tides off the Ferry with old Sonny, but for thirty years or so Kiltearn was the centre of activity. In many ways it's a great place to fish. The view is very fine: all the usual sights from the firth – the checkerboard fields and woods of the Black Isle to the south, Easter Ross and the Sutors in the distance to the east and the Ross-shire hills away to the west – but also a great vantage point from which to admire Ben Wyvis and the Munro lands. Hector, our landlord and the chief of the clan, when he came fishing with us, would particularly enjoy the prospect of his woods and barley fields – that is, when he was not taking off, as on a famous occasion, to chase an escaping grilsie on foot up the shallow bed of the Skiach, before catching it in his hands. Nearer at hand is the roofless kirk of Kiltearn, surrounded by the fine old yews of its graveyard. Here lie many family, friends and fellow fishermen. Stan is here, well named 'Armstrong', a bull of a man in strength yet the kindest fellow you could meet, and devoted to the fishing. Doug is here too. My father, mother and brother are here. And, of course, very many Munros are here, from clan chiefs to working Highlanders.

It is all low-water fishing at Kiltearn. When Dave, Rik and Steve fished it long ago they would row back and forth from the little beach below Balachladdich. The fishing off the beach itself wasn't great, although it is a haunt of sea trout and an occasional head passes by. Big Rik once had a shot of a dozen or so on his own here – an easier feat for someone of his giant stature and strength. When Doug took on Kiltearn he established a mooring on the inside cairn, and we would leave the boat on it at the end of the tide. This was convenient in some ways – no tractor and trailer required, just a five-minute walk from the kirkyard car park across the ebb – but it could cause problems. If you were late for the tide, the boat could be aground. More than once I have found myself running down the shore (not easy in waders and oilskin jacket), then having to throw the net off the boat to lighten her enough to haul her, swearing and sweating, off the mud and into the water.

More serious were the occasions when the boat broke free from her mooring. This happened three times, in every case down to a westerly gale. Twice we were saved by the pipeline pier, which caught her and stopped her from sailing on to Invergordon or

Wading out to the boat on her mooring.

out through the Sutors. On one of these occasions, Rod and I rowed her back in the middle of the night, to catch the flood tide. It was a memorable trip: the water was rough, and it was dark enough for us not always to be sure where we were. When we got to Kiltearn, Rod went home and I stayed with the boat, sheltering in the whins until it got light, with only the odd rabbit for company, and occasionally walking down to the water to push her out and keep her afloat as the tide ebbed, until eventually the mooring was uncovered. The fiercest gale of the lot – unprecedented in summertime – came a few years ago when I was away for the weekend, staying with Eddie on the Isle of Eigg. Of course, she broke free again, but this time, thank goodness, it was at half-tide, and she caught on one of the big tree trunks brought down by a winter spate in the Skiach. It was a hell of a mess – boat capsized, net strung out, duckboards floated away. But two good souls, Rod and Steve K, were on the scene promptly and got young Finnian to bring a front-loader down to the rescue. At least the boat herself had suffered no injury, the boat rope had held, the net was intact and the oars were safe up at Keith's. There was technically another week to go that season, but we hadn't the heart to carry on. In later years the mooring, which used to be a long metal ground screw driven into the cairn and which the last gale had simply uprooted, was replaced by an enormous iron link half buried in the mud and secured to the boat with a stout chain.

For a dozen years or so I fished Kiltearn with Doug. I was already living away in England, teaching, but the fishing season coincided conveniently with my summer holidays, and I spent every July on the firth. Doug was a one-off. We first knew him when he appeared at the bothy back in the old days. We, the Balconie Babes, were

Doug with his sons, Liam (left) and Struan. (*FC*)

Doug (3rd right) at work. In the background (L to R) Andy, Old Paul and I are piling the net. (*FC*)

pseudo-hippies in those days, strictly green tea, weed and macrobiotic food, and Doug, a bit older, with his tattoos, gappy teeth and cans of Special Brew, came as a bit of a shock. But it soon became clear that despite the rough exterior and the extraordinary accent, combined of equal parts the Broch (Fraserburgh), Lancashire and Essex, he was really a great big huggy bear and, just as important, a dedicated fisherman. Steve K reminded me recently of how we all met. He and Doug were working on the restoration of Foulis Castle at the time, and we were in the middle of the fishing season.

'It was a weekend party at Woodlands, and these two characters [Eddie and I] turned up, very sunburned and with a faraway look in their eyes. Then they mentioned fishing, and Doug and I were down the bothy the next chance we had.'

Steve also let on that he thought at first Eddie and I might be a couple. Couple of chancers, more like.

Doug could turn his hands to most things in the building line, and he had a remarkable back story, episodes from which emerged during the long hours in the boat at Kiltearn when not much else was happening. 'Did I tell you about when I played drums with Lonnie Donegan?' 'Did I tell you about the time I was cast adrift in an open boat in the Caribbean with a crate of Guinness and a packet of cocktail pork sausages?' He had been on trawlers, he had been a gamekeeper, he had run fruit machines in London, he had been inside. Years ago, before the fishing days, Eddie had encountered him in London when he appeared at the door as hired muscle to recover some stolen property. When the fishing was slow, it would be, 'It'll never catch on as a spectator sport' and 'Nil bleedin' desperandum, as my old grandpappy used to say'. Then he would treat us to renditions of Hits of the Fifties and 'I Do Like to be Beside the Seaside'. We sang that at his funeral, beside the firth. His grave ('Gone Fishing') looks straight out at the cairns.

Some of those Kiltearn years were quite productive. I recall once or twice packing the old van with a few boxes to go the Bannerman's, the fish merchant in Tain. And there were still good heads knocking about – big black peaks heading up from Balconie through the shallows towards the inside cairn and then cutting out, but not too far for us to get round them; or jumps down in the bay developing into nice-looking swims following the strips of fresh in the current up to the outside cairn. Double-figure shots – tens, twenties, even thirties. But latterly there were also some desperately poor years. Long blank tides, blank days, even a blank week or two – a taste of what was to come.

It wasn't always easy to find crew. At a pinch, we could manage with just the two of us, one in the boat and one on the cairn; but it is much handier to have two in the boat, and the time passes much quicker if you have someone to chew the fat with, especially

A crowded cairn. (*RR*)

when not much else is happening. Evening tides were rarely a problem – there were plenty people happy to come fishing after work, sometimes too many, in fact. The cairn could get crowded at times. Early mornings weren't so easy, but Doug usually managed to locate somebody – student, schoolboy, unemployed or pensioner. In particular, he had two faithful female hands, a pair of lovely sisters; with their high colour, freckles, curly hair and sparkling eyes, they could have come straight off a 'Visit the Highlands' poster. Then there was old Paul the Pole, now retired from the distillery, a most agreeable fishing companion, even if not above giving a sly pinch to the girls. He didn't say much but he had a wicked sense of humour, he knew the job and he was absolutely reliable. Arriving in Scotland at the end of the war, he had been quickly collared by Aggie, who was evidently worried about being left on the shelf. We asked him once, 'When did you marry Aggie, Paul?' and he replied, 'I no marry Aggie. Aggie marry me!'

Doug's death came out of the blue, just a few weeks before the first season of the twenty-first century. On a fencing job near home, he picked up the mell to knock in a stob, dropped it and was dead before it hit the ground.

I fished for just a couple of weeks that season, but we still had nearly fifty fish. With Doug gone, I was now in charge again, and in subsequent years we fished for about a month. It wasn't always easy being 500 miles away for most of the year. For a start, there was cairn maintenance. Back in the day, the cairns used to be pushed up every year, at Alness, Balconie and Kiltearn, during the really big tides in March or April. This was a job for Angie, the Estate bulldozer driver, a short, stocky fellow with a cap over one eye and a pipe in the corner of his mouth – Popeye to the life, and wonderfully nimble on the dance floor when it came to a ceilidh. He knew the job like the back of his hand: mounding the sand and gravel, running over it time and again to firm it, then tapering the front of the cairn where the shot is landed. The bulldozer would often turn up huge, pink, wriggling ragworms almost two feet long, and birds we never saw during the summer would appear – notably, one year, a flight of delicate kittiwakes, silvery in the early spring sunshine. Of course, wind, wave and current will flatten cairns eventually, but the years of work gave them a solid base, including some big stones, and they have never disappeared. The Kiltearn cairns were pushed up only twice in my time – once, at considerable expense, by Vince, a professional brought in specially; and the second time, for just £50 in his hand, by the son of a friend who happened to be at the shore on another job with earth-moving machinery at precisely the right time to catch one of the biggest tides.

Some cairns never needed attention. The Bell at Alness is made of big stones which never shift, and then there is the Slippery Stones at Kiltearn. Along with the Big Cairn at Balconie and the Bell, this must be an ancient foundation, probably put there to anchor one end of a net in the days before 'fixed engines' were banned in the firth. And it certainly is slippery – the broad blades of kelp covering its big flat stones are smooth and slick, and no one who has regularly tried to stand on it will have escaped a tumble. I once fished a tide there with Buller and his pal Willie, an old boy with a wooden leg who spent much of the time on his back. It's a good place to fish, however, when it comes up on a big tide, and it provides a home for many small marine creatures – pipefish, blennies, sticklebacks and crabs; we have even found small octopus there, and not surprisingly, it's a favourite stance for the heron.

The net was another worry. You had to have a fairly long one at Kiltearn, and Doug had been using a big old thing which was very heavy. Young Jodie, a keen fisherman for a few seasons, had an acquaintance in Avoch on the Black Isle who remade the net for us, putting in a new bag and some new sheets. She was still a heavy pull, though – or perhaps we were getting older. Five or six years ago, Rod, Jonathan and I replaced some of the tattiest sheets with new material, and a

Two grilsies on the Slippery Stones.

Doug and his boys working on a net. (*FC*)

Nil Desperandum in better days. (*FC*)

couple of years ago I bit the bullet and ordered a new net. I couldn't find a supplier in Scotland, so ended up with a netmaker in Bridport, Dorset. Rod, the genial boss, was a little surprised at an order for a salmon sweep net – 'We haven't made one of them in a long while' – but he had some 4″ mesh stuff going cheap. I supplied a brand new bag, which Steve K had been hoarding for years, and the whole deal was pretty reasonable. The net worked like a dream and was a breeze to pull, although as it turned out, we only used it for a week. But that's another story.

Then there was the coble. It's asking a lot of a wooden boat to spend just a few weeks a year in the water – boards dry out and crack – and the coble Doug used, *Nil Desperandum*, was well past her best. When the Alness and Balconie fishings came to an end, all the other cobles – the *Buller*, the *Balconie Lady*, the *Bonus* and the *Mary Jane*, had ended up on dry land as tourist attractions, parked on the shore beside the girnel at Foulis Ferry. The description of the *Buller*, which I wrote and which was pinned on her, reads:

This boat was named for James 'Buller' Black, for many years a salmon fisher on the Cromarty Firth. Buller learned to fish, and learned in particular the art of spotting fish, from his grandfather, who worked the salmon fishings at the mouth of the Alness/Averon river between the wars. Buller also fished at other stations, including Tarbat, the mouth of the Conon and the Crown fishings in Alness Bay. In the early 1960s he returned to full-time fishing when Munro-Ferguson of Novar reopened his stations at Balconie and Alness. Buller passed on his skills to a later generation of fishermen, some of whom are still fishing in the Firth today. The boat was built by McCuish Brothers of Inverness to Buller's specifications for fishing the Alness station. It was designed to carry a crew of up to six men and transport considerable quantities of salmon – a catch of several hundred fish on a single tide was not unusual at that time.

Tourist attractions. The name plates were painted by Fionna Chalmers. (*FC*)

The *Buller* and the other cobles on shore were deteriorating fast. In fact, they were beginning to break up and would eventually have to be burned. But I reckoned it might not be too late to save the best of them. The *Balconie Lady* is a typical small coble and a lovely boat to work: stable when you are standing in her at anchor, as we often are, and sturdy enough to take the inevitable grinding on the stones of the cairn, yet responsive to manoeuvre and fast to row.

Strong and well made though she is, the years on shore had not been kind to the *Lady*. In her twenty years at Kiltearn she underwent two major repair jobs: the first was undertaken by a boat-builder in Ullapool, who replaced some boards and sections of the

Steve K with *Balconie Lady* under repair.

gunwale; the second, more extensive work after a clumsy moving job with a front-loader had stove in her bow, was beautifully executed by Brian Knox and Steve K. In between times, there were seasons when she leaked like a sieve – lots of bailing required, and the odd morning early on, before her timbers had swollen in the water, when I came down to find her sunk at the mooring, the net streaming down towards Invergordon. Regular maintenance and painting, essential to keep her seaworthy, was tricky to arrange, but for many years it was taken care of by Kit Kennedy, who invariably did an immaculate job on her.

With limited time at my disposal, and not wishing to leave Jan, still working then, for a long period in the summer, it wasn't easy to decide which weeks to fish. Our impression was that the grilse run, insofar as it still existed,

Big Rik.

now came rather later, so we tended to start in mid-July and fish on into August. This didn't always produce results. As it always was with the fishing, if you are not there all the time you may miss those crucial tides or that couple of big heads which can make your season. Because it seemed, as the grilse declined, that the early fish might be on the up, we twice tried fishing a couple of weeks in May. One May was a write-off – filthy weather and no fish – but the other saw some success which slightly backfired on us. We had three lovely big springers and a good sea trout in the back of the boat, when the bailiffs, no doubt surprised to see us on the water, paid us a visit, the first for many years. I could see them looking at the silver beauties with longing and hatred in their eyes – longing to have them up the river for the rods, and hatred for the netsmen who had intercepted them. I am convinced that this encounter contributed to our eventual removal.

For a good many years, until his bad leg began to trouble him, I had the good fortune of having big Rik – the 'human winch' – as my regular companion on the water. You couldn't have asked for a better one. Great strength, of course, but also endless curiosity about the world, great sensitivity to all its beauties, a rare imagination and a finely developed sense of humour. One calm warm day in the boat, when very little else was happening, the ebb started to bring a long procession of jellyfish past us – purple moon jellies, not the big 'scalders'. Watching them became quite hypnotic (we may have smoked a joint or two), and as they pulsed in and out I said to Rik,

Familiar faces. Rik holds up a grilse to a big crew on the last day of the season. (*RR*)

'There's something almost sexual about the way they move, isn't there?' Just then, two particularly fine specimens floated into view, vibrating away. 'Mmm', said Rik, checking them out, 'I don't fancy yours much.'

It was a fair journey to the fishing for Rik from his Sutherland fastness – always on two wheels of course, and roe deer pose a significant risk to the motorcyclist on small

Back on dry land. Self, Rik, Jonathan. (*RR*)

Rod on the outside cairn.

Highland roads in the early morning – but he was never late for a tide. And the second half of his journey, over Struie Hill and then on the A9, gave him plenty of opportunity to open the throttle as he loves to do.

The 'Rik years', as I think of them, were pretty good ones on the whole. Many familiar faces showed up at the fishing, and though we never caught that many fish – we didn't actually want to catch a lot – there were usually enough to keep the crew happy, give some to friends and relations and leave a few over for the smoker. For several years I sold smoked fish to my school colleagues at Christmas and made enough to cover some of the costs of the operation.

Sadly, there came a time when Rik could no longer get to the fishing. But fortunately, this pretty much coincided with another first mate retiring from his day job and becoming available full time. I have known Rod since boyhood – our mothers were friends – and he had been an occasional fisherman for many years. So he knew the job and, just as importantly, he was excellent company in the boat. Our talk ranged over politics, cricket (we once played for the same team, and Rod was still playing into his sixties) and family history. Rod usually had a good dram about him, and we would both revert to smoking for the duration of the season.

In these later years it wasn't as easy as it had once been to find crew. Many of the old faces had faded out, moved away or lost interest. Hardly surprising, when so pitifully few fish were now being caught. But one willing hand re-emerged in the shape of Jonathan. A pal of Stevie Web's from Wick, he had come to the fishing in the old Balconie days, but

Jonathan.

I hadn't seen him for years. Another one who knew the job, Jonathan is a patient, good-natured fellow – the perfect man to round out the crew.

For many of these Kiltearn years I had the great good fortune of being able to stay right on the spot. Keith, an old friend who quite often came out to the fishing himself, kindly offered me a room for the season in his house, which is scarcely ten minutes' walk from the cairns. After the tide, the crew would often gather there, and it became a sort of informal bothy. I took to leaving the boat there in the winters – parked upside down outdoors, the correct way to store a wooden boat so that it neither dries out nor collects water. In one of life's strange coincidences, Keith sold his house and moved away at exactly the same time that Marine Scotland brought the fishing to an end. It was obviously meant to be.

Keith's place. 'The finest fishing bothy in Scotland'.

Floating out to the cairn. (L to R) Keith, self, Rod. (*JH*)

The boat turned over for the winter. (L to R) self, Youssuf, Daniel, Rik. (*RR*)

29

The Last Good Tide

It depends on what you call 'a good tide', of course. Once upon a time, the morning I am going to describe would have been nothing special; in high season, it would have been passable at Kiltearn, slightly disappointing at Balconie, very poor at Alness. But almost ten years ago at Kiltearn, when it happened, it was a red-letter day.

There was a good crew out in the morning: Rod, a regular by this time, and Oz, an old friend of the fishing. They were supplemented by a visitor, a young South African, who had been a little taken aback when I told him I would be calling for him at 3.45 am, but who turned out to be a strong and willing hand.

It was one of those mornings when everything went right. To begin with it was calm, then we got a nice little breeze

(L to R) Oz, Rod, self, with the kirkyard wall behind us.

from the west, not too strong. It was warm but not too bright. The tide was just a perfect size, big enough for us to get on to the outside cairn but not so big as to make the water awkwardly shallow.

When fish did come, it was what now counted as a little shottie – seven of them. In subsequent years, I don't believe we ever had a shot of more than three. And that wasn't the end of it. We had several more shots, no blanks, and ended the tide with seventeen fish. Carrying them up the beach was no picnic.

Our South African friend took some convincing that the fishing wasn't always like this, and he was delighted to take a grilsie away to give to his hosts. The crew got a couple each, I was able to pay my dues in fish to my family and my landlords, and there were a couple of donkeys, too, just right for the smoker.

30

The Biologists

When we were fishing Kiltearn, not long after Doug's death, I was contacted by the Freshwater Fisheries Laboratory at Faskally near Pitlochry, somewhere I have never visited, although I have driven past it countless times and enjoyed the sign 'Dam and Fish Ladder' – words I sometimes considered employing as a fisherman's curse when we had a bad blank. Anyway, they were planning to conduct a study of the movement of fish in estuarial waters and wanted to know if we could help. This would involve three biologists spending a week with us, tagging a certain number of the fish we caught, fitting them with electronic transmitters, releasing them and monitoring their movements.

The biologists duly arrived, a chief and two young assistants. The chief was a rather buttoned-up fellow but reasonably friendly, and the two young chaps were likely lads, promising to be good company on the cairn and useful hands on a rope. They were looking for twenty fish, and would compensate us for any they tagged. I told them that we were highly unlikely to have that many to spare – catches were already well down at this date – but that I had a cunning plan: if we could secure permission to fish a few tides at Balconie (unfished for more than a decade and now owned by the District Fishery Board), I was pretty sure we could get them what they needed. They got permission from the Board without difficulty, and I marked down a couple of big morning tides which should be good for the sandbank. The idea of being back at Balconie was exciting, and I anticipated a few nice shotties as in the old days. But now I made a big mistake: once they had the fish they needed, I thought that we would be able to keep some for ourselves, and with a nod and a wink I said to the chief biologist something like, 'I expect there'll be a few damaged fish which we'll have to knock on the head.' He appeared to take this on board, I believed we had come to an understanding and I told the crew.

The biologists' first task was to set out buoyed receivers at a dozen points in the inner firth and in the mouth of the Conon, Black Rock and Skiach rivers which would pick up the signals given out by the transmitters in the fish. This done, they came out with us to the Kiltearn cairns to test their equipment. There was the tackle required to actually tag the fish, but also two big black plastic tanks, about the size of a household cistern, which they filled with water from the firth. When we caught a fish, it was quickly put into Tank 1, which contained an anaesthetic (a derivative of cocaine, we were entertained to learn). After a few minutes, once the fish had calmed down, it was taken out, tagged and had its 'magic bullet' transmitter inserted. This was an alarming

Rik with the two junior biologists. The water looks a bit too calm for fishing. (*RR*)

procedure. The fish's mouth was held open by one biologist while another injected down its throat a cartridge about the size of my thumb. Then the fish was put into Tank 2, which contained clean water, until it recovered. I imagine that the technology has now moved on (this was almost twenty years ago) and that the process is now a lot less invasive – in fact it must be, since smolts, a fraction of the size of a grilse, are now being monitored in this way. And in fact, not all the fish survived it; I recall two fatalities.

After a couple of days it became obvious that Kiltearn was not going to produce the fish they needed, so we made preparations to go down to the Balconie bank the next day. There was no difficulty collecting a crew for this venture, and we set off mob-handed – the three biologists, Rik, Oz, Rod and I. We were in two boats, and we borrowed an outboard to fit on the coble (the backboard is cut to take an engine, although we very rarely used one).

It was great to be back on the bank. Nothing much had changed, but although conditions were fine, there wasn't much to be seen. Finally, fish did appear, a typically close shot of eight. Fine, I thought, four fish for them and four for us, and I asked Rik to throw a killing stick over.

'No, no, no!' the chief biologist cried, and all my plans went up in smoke. It suddenly became clear that he had not understood our unspoken agreement, and he was going to stick to the letter of the law – the fish were the River Board's, not ours.

This was a facer, but there was nothing I could do about it. He had the law on his side, and I had no wish to be reported to the Board. All the crew looked pretty glum, but Rik took it particularly badly, stumping off up the bank, sitting on the sand with his back to us and taking no further part in the morning – I think we may have had one other shot. I could see that he was fuming and was only relieved that he had not thumped the guy. Rik has a temper, and if he thumps you, you are going to stay thumped. I have seen him pick up a chap who was misbehaving at a dance, carry him out of the hall as you or I might carry a shopping basket and throw him in the gutter.

The rest of that day and the remaining few days that the biologists were with us were distinctly awkward. We didn't go back to the bank, they got a few more fish at Kiltearn and eventually they offered to buy us a dozen fish to compensate for the fishing time we had lost – Rik refused to take any, I was not so proud. But they still hadn't got all the fish they needed, so I took them to a high water at Balconie, and sure enough, we had a classic beach shot of nine fish which filled their quota.

And the results of their research? The final conclusion with regard to the movement of fish in the firth was, 'No consistent overall pattern emerged.' It came as no surprise to me that most of the tagged fish swam up and down the firth with no fixed pattern to their movements, although they tended to move towards the Conon on the flood tide and away from it on the ebb. Four fish left the area completely and another was caught in a net at the mouth of the Ness. Several entered the Conon, one of which then left it and entered the Black Rock. All of this confirmed my belief that fish move around all the firths and my observation that they sometimes swim with the tide and sometimes against it. We could have told them that before they even started.

31

The Other Fishers

When you stand in a little boat or on a cairn for an hour, two hours, three hours without moving much, the other fishers in the firth begin to accept you as part of the scenery.

Most like us are the herons, who stand in wait at the edge of the ebb with their spears at the ready. This is why I chose a heron for my tobacco tin, beautifully painted by Fionna Chalmers but sadly lost. Although I would guess that they are rarely persecuted nowadays, the herons of the firth are still wary of man and normally unwilling to come within gunshot. It is a privilege, therefore, to watch them standing on the Slippery Stones, or stalking the shallows only twenty yards or so from us.

The most exciting fisher is the osprey, cruising above the shallows then crashing down in a flurry of spray to nail a sea trout or flounder. When I was first at the fishing, ospreys had not long returned to Scotland and to see one you had to make a special trip to Loch Garten. Now there are at least 250 pairs and they are a common sight on the firth, although so striking that we still comment on their appearance, especially if they

Osprey overhead.

A cormorant
taking fright.

fly directly over our heads, as they often do. Doug was the first fisherman to spot one. We used to keep a telescope at the bothy in the old days, and scanning the Black Isle shore one day he let out an exclamation of astonishment. We all had a look, and sure enough, it was an osprey, perched dramatically on the ruinous roof of Castlecraig. Now a pair nests regularly at the top of a big pine on that shore.

Cormorants – 'black jocks' to us, one of Buller's names – pound purposefully up and down the firth at wave height and sometimes alight to swim and dive in the channel. The marks which they and their fellow divers the mergansers make are often a distraction when we are watching for fish on a calm day. Occasionally we see a cormorant wrestling with an eel near the river mouth, but most of their fishing takes place out in the deep. They are wary of us and will veer off if they find themselves heading for the boat or the cairn. Believing that West Highlanders of old used to relish 'sea turkey', Dave J and I tried stewed cormorant one day. I wouldn't recommend it. A much better meal was once supplied by a greylag goose; Dave and I spotted that it couldn't fly, pursued it in the boat and shot it with the .22. I cannot imagine doing such a thing now, but we were wilder men in those days.

The terns are the fishers who work closest to us: at high water, when the boat at Kiltearn was riding at her mooring hundreds of yards from the beach they sometimes used her as a perch, and we found the bow white with their droppings. Often they would mob the boat and screech at us when we took over. At low water, when we are fishing, these sea swallows hunt the shoreline beside us, so light and delicate in flight that each wing beat seems to bounce them upwards, then suddenly braking and hovering, head absolutely still, before darting down to pluck a sand eel from the water. Late in the season, we often see young birds pursuing their parents down the firth, screaming for food.

Many of the birds who hunt at low water seek their prey on the long stretch of weed, mud, sand and pebbles exposed by the ebb. There is usually a redshank or two knocking about and occasionally some ringed plovers. Curlews are in trouble in much of the UK, but not here. The soundtrack to every morning or evening tide includes their bubbling calls, and just last year, in late August, I saw a flight of about fifty when

Common tern.

walking at Balconie Point. (Having written 'flight' I looked up the collective noun for curlews and found it to be 'herd' – perhaps a reflection of their size, as the largest wader.) In August we begin to see passage migrants on the water: a flash of dunlin and sometimes a more stately flight of bar-tailed godwits or whimbrel.

Oystercatchers, the most characteristic of the firth's wading birds, are my favourites. Their piping calls sometimes run together to become a trilling song, and when they take off from the musselbanks to fly across the water on a pale grey day the white on their wings seems to glow as if fluorescent. One of the first signs of the Highland spring is hearing them at night in the fields above.

Oystercatchers feeding.

Gulls are always with us, and always on the lookout for food. If you toss the crust of your piece in the water, a herring gull or common gull will appear from nowhere and scoop it up. All the birds of the shore give way to the greater black-backs, and everyone looks up nervously at the hoarse, almost canine yelps which announce their arrival. Then the black-backs, just one or two, plane down, deliberately making for a stretch of shore where there are plenty of birds, in order to assert their dominance and create the maximum disturbance and terror. You just know that if the worst happened and you stepped off into deep water in your waders and drowned, the black-backs would be the first to have your eyes. One morning, Rik and I spotted a low-level chase taking place in the distance. As the two birds got closer, we saw that it was a mallard duck being pursued by a greater black-backed gull. Normally, you would expect a mallard to be able to outpace a black-back easily, but this one was hot on the tail of its prey, chasing it like some gigantic falcon. The gull must have spotted that the duck was not a strong flyer. The pair passed us, going like smoke, then a hundred yards away the duck made the fatal mistake of landing on the water. Straight away the black-back was on to her, grabbed her before she could dive and drowned her. The last we saw of them, as the flood tide took them away towards the west, was the black-back starting to pluck its prize.

These big gulls are formidable predators. When rabbits were plentiful around Kiltearn, we often saw the birds patrolling the shoreline, quartering the ground almost like hen harriers, looking to pick up unwary young bunnies. At Alness a heartrending scene was played out in front of Dalmore cairn one morning, when two black-backs cornered a merganser which for some reason was unable to fly. Now mergansers are expert divers, and this one was using all its underwater skill to escape the gulls' attentions. When it popped up, the black-backs were on to it; then it would dive, stay

Greater black-backed gull – 'a formidable predator'.

Red-breasted
merganser.

down as long as possible and come up some yards away, whereupon the black-backs
would spot it and return to the attack. This grim ballet went on for twenty minutes or
more, but the gulls were not about to give up, and eventually the inevitable happened:
the merganser ran out of puff, failed to dive in time and the black-backs got it. They
seized a wing each and literally tore the poor thing apart.

The duck population of the firth has undergone quite a few changes in the years
I have known it. The mergansers are still doing well. We often see their streamlined
shapes racing past in low flight – the fighter jets of the bird world – or spot large
families swimming out from the river mouths, and they seem to have benefited from
the healthy populations of fry in the firth. Goosanders don't appear to breed here, but
we have seen the occasional one during the season. Mallard continue to be common,
and large parties are often seen in August. Shelduck are less common than they once
were, however, perhaps because there is more human disturbance along the shore where
they used to nest; once we would see really big multi-family crèches of ducklings, but
no more. The biggest change has been the welcome arrival of eiders, a bird I had never
seen in the firth before the start of the twenty-first century. We almost never see a
drake, but broods of eiders have become a familiar sight – not surprisingly, perhaps,
given the firth's good population of mussels, their favourite food. Of course, I am
talking about the firth in summer. In winter it's a very different story. Wigeon are then
the dominant species, with occasional goldeneye and sometimes blow-ins like long-
tailed ducks and scoters.

Another change has been the arrival of summer geese. There has been a population
of Canadas on the Beauly Firth for some time, but in the last fifteen years or so our
fishing has been accompanied by almost a hundred of them. They are far from wild,
and will often swim through the back of the cairn between us and the shore, less than
20 yards away. The flock often contains an outlier or two – a bar-headed goose on one

Seals on the sandbank.

occasion, and several barnacle geese, as well as a number of greylags. My impression is that the resident greylag population has greatly increased in recent years, and they have certainly bred in the hinterland of Balconie Point. I have several times seen families of goslings on the water there.

The osprey is the only fish-eating raptor that we see, although I live in hope of seeing a sea eagle over the firth one day – a reasonable expectation, since Scotland is now home to well over a hundred pairs. Plenty of other raptors visit us, however. Buzzards and red kites both float over the water on occasion, and once in a while a sparrowhawk or peregrine wings its way across. Just once, at the end of the season, a male hen harrier appeared, like a white ghost, quartering the Balconie fields. I have twice seen peregrines take prey at the shore during the season, although they are commoner there in the winter. I had just walked round the back of the bothy one day when a small party of starlings took off from the trees. Big mistake on their part, for suddenly a peregrine hit them. They scattered like shrapnel, but not before he had grabbed one, in a burst of feathers, and made off towards the river. Another time, fishing at Alness, a peregrine appeared flying low over the pebbles of the beach. There were a number of waders there, oystercatchers and lapwings, and they all had the sense to crouch down low to the ground. One foolish half-grown chick, however, stood up and peered around to see what was happening. The peregrine scarcely checked his flight, just dropped a little lower and plucked it off the beach like a gardener dead-heading a rose.

Our companion in the water is the seal – 'Charlie' to many fishermen but always 'Henry' to us. There are many common (harbour) seals in the firth. They haul out on the big sandbanks to the west of us, where they have their pups in the early summer, and they work the channel when the fish are running. Occasionally we see Henry take a fish, head out of the water and shaking it like a terrier with a rat.

Sometimes we used to find a seal or two hauled out on the Balconie sandbank when we arrived to fish low water. They were clearly curious about us and would rear up for a good look, before shuffling off back into the water. Seals are known to like music, and one day we took a piper of our acquaintance out to play to them. They showed a lot of interest in him. Some years ago, a research programme required the scientists involved to capture a number of seals in the firth. Apparently (I never witnessed it), their technique was to race up in a fast boat to a sandbank where seals were hauled out, then jump out of the boat and surround one with net. This can't have been easy. These seals can be up to six feet long and may weigh well over 100kg. And they have sharp teeth; a seal's skull could easily be mistaken for that of a big dog or even a wolf.

One season at Kiltearn, Rik and I were haunted for several days by a very young seal pup which had clearly lost its mother. It would swim up close to us crying piteously, and eventually we spotted it stranded on the edge of the ebb in Kiltearn bay. What to do? We rowed across to it, killing sticks at the ready and prepared to put it out of its misery. But when we got there, its pleading eyes were too much for us. After a lengthy discussion of the ethical issues involved, we decided that we could only kill it if we were going to then eat it, or at least use its skin. This we didn't fancy, so we ended up carrying it back to the water and relaunching it. We never saw it again, and I would be very surprised if it survived.

Our relationship with Henry is a complicated one: often we curse him, when we see what looks like a big shot of fish coming towards us, only for the shiny black seal head to pop up instead; time was we would put a .22 bullet over it to scare him away. But if the seal is there, the chance is the fish are too, so an occasional appearance is welcome. He is curious about us and will often come in close for a look, and we usually greet him as a familiar. Both parties recognize a certain kinship.

32

Poached Salmon

Poaching in the river is one thing – netting a pool, snagging fish with a 'ripper' or even poisoning the water with Cymag (sodium cyanide) or the like. I know little of this, although we did once briefly consider trying a pool with a sack of ragwort, said to be an effective herbal killer of fish. Salt-water poaching we do know something of, however. Here and there along the firth, especially on the less populated Black Isle shore, the odd illegal net was always set. We knew of one that lived under a little upturned fibreglass boat hidden in the bushes near Castlecraig, opposite the bothy. On the whole, poachers would keep away from the bits of shore where we fished – in this way, we acted as kind of unofficial bailiffs – but once or twice, when fishing first light at Kiltearn, we saw suspicious characters walking away from Balconie Point.

The Fishery Management Plan published in 2008 by the Cromarty Firth Fishery Board and the Cromarty Firth Fishery Trust contained an interesting section on poaching in the firth:

> Poaching has long been seen as a significant impact on the stocks of migratory fish in the Cromarty Firth region. In 1895 the DAFS 'Salmon Fisheries of Scotland' Report states that because of the extent of illegal netting by Cromarty fishermen, 'I fear that the Alness will by-and-by cease to be a sea trout river.' In 1977 George Macintosh's Superintendent's report to the Conon Board states, 'This has been a very poor year for salmon, in fact they appear to be getting less every year. Everyone who owns a boat is after them. I don't think the day is far distant when the only salmon to be found will be on fish farms' … Illegal coastal netting became an even more serious threat with the development of mono-filament gill nets which could be easily concealed and also catch large numbers of salmon. [There was a] war of attrition which the Conon Bailiffs have waged against coastal gill netting … [involving a] level of intimidation, violence and vandalism …

Salmon netting is governed by a host of laws and regulations, both national and local. With an occasional exception, as described elsewhere – toot and haul on a misty morning, long, *very* slow shots at Nigg, some throwing of stones – we always abided by the law. But not everyone did. The Management Plan continues:

As well as gill netting there has been a history of illegal operation of net and coble at netting stations in the Moray Firth area. The DAFS 'Salmon Fisheries of Scotland' report for 1904 describes three methods in which sweep nets were being operated in the Cromarty Firth to illegally increase their efficiency by turning them into fixed engines. [See Chapter 2, Catching the Fish] This problem still exists and in recent years the Board has sent copies of current legislation, which very clearly defines the legal method of net and coble operation, to all netting proprietors. This has been backed up with warnings given to netsmen and by several successful prosecutions both in the Cromarty Firth and in joint operations with the Ness DSFB in the neighbouring firth.

I have in front of me a copy of the District Fishery Board's letter referred to above. It quotes some clauses from the *Salmon (Definition of Methods of Net Fishing and Construction of Nets) (Scotland) Regulations 1992* which it summarizes as follows:

> The legislation clearly states that the net must not be allowed to remain stationary, and therefore the practice of running out a net and leaving it stationary whilst bringing a rope attached to the end of the net back to shore is not legal.

This is a good description of the way some 'banging' stations work their nets. I have quite often seen them at it. But of course, the regulation is open to interpretation. Only on very rare occasions do we leave a net stationary on purpose; but what if we see fish, have some net pulled off, and then the fish disappear? We will stop rowing, stand up to scan the water, and the net becomes stationary. Or what is the position when we row a very wide shot and run out of net long before the boat gets back to the cairn. Again, the net is effectively stationary until we can start to pull it in. Are we breaking the law? I don't believe so. Because we can spot fish and row our shot precisely to intercept them, it is in our interest to keep the net moving and close it up as quickly as possible.

Gill nets, those disgusting things, are a different matter. The Board's letter goes on to say:

> The legislation further states that the net must not be designed to catch fish by enmeshing them. This means that no section of gill net may be included in the net construction, whether it is monofilament or multi-strand.

Again, this is open to interpretation. The nets we used at Nigg had a larger mesh size (4½″ as opposed to 3½″) and some of the wings were of fairly thin twine; consequently, they did gill fish quite often. And even the 3½″ mesh of the nets we used at Alness, Balconie and Kiltearn occasionally gilled fish. We didn't *want* to gill them – in fact they were a nuisance; getting them out of the net is time-consuming, and a gilled fish looks damaged. But were these fish illegally caught?

From the Management Plan again:

During the 1990s a concerted effort was made to combat illegal gill netting. Coastal patrols were increased in frequency, collaboration and information sharing with neighbouring Boards was developed and helicopter patrols funded by the Scottish Fishery Protection Agency were used. This resulted in increased net seizures for several years and a period of confrontation with poachers. There were a number of assaults on bailiffs, damage to property and vehicles, threats of violence involving firearms and threatened poisoning of rivers. A significant turning point in the campaign against gill netting came from the designation of the Inner Moray Firth as an SAC [Special Area of Conservation] for bottle-nosed dolphins. Entanglement in illegal gill nets was identified as a significant preventable cause of dolphin mortality. A campaign called 'Operation Fishnet' was launched to raise public awareness of the environmental damage caused by gill netting. It also gave a 'hot line' to report illegal netting. The effect of this has been to turn public opinion against illegal netting and encourage the courts to deal with poachers more rigorously, treating salmon poaching as wildlife crime.

Three cheers for that.

Now that virtually all legal salmon netting has ceased, there is effectively no official market in Scotland for wild salmon. This doesn't mean that some do not get taken, as they say, for the pot. But the days of what might be called 'commercial' poaching have gone.

A beautiful cock fish for the smoker.

33

A Kiltearn Morning

It is one of those mornings when I get up in the dark, soon after three o'clock. One of the biggest tides of the season is coming, and I don't want to risk getting down to the cairn and finding the boat aground. Stumble out of bed in my narrow little room at Keith's, splash the face, put the kettle on and sit down to a bowl of muesli topped with Kiltearn strawberries. Keith's strawberry plants, Cambridge Late Pine, a delicious old-fashioned variety, originally came from Achandunie, my family's home. Fill my flask, with tea, no milk, two sugars and a good squirt of lemon juice. Get my piece, made the night before, out of the fridge – two rolls filled with ham, cheddar, tomato and mustard – and pick up a nectarine and a Tunnock caramel wafer to go with them.

Now check my bag – have I got everything? Piece, flask, hip flask (Glenmorangie), tobacco, lighter, knife, binoculars, netting needle, scarf, cap, tide book, polaroids. Then get dressed: work trousers, but no long johns today (it is July, after all), thin socks and woollen stockings over them, T-shirt, flannel shirt, fleece waistcoat, fishing sweater (an oiled wool Norwegian job, a present from my Orkney godmother and never been washed, it can be seen in many of the photographs in this book). Two more layers are waiting in the car, a fleece jacket and a waterproof. This may seem excessive, but out on the cairn there is absolutely no shelter from the wind. A pleasant summer's day on land can be a different story when you are standing out in the middle of the firth with a stiff easterly blowing. And as we say, if you've got it you can always take it off; but if you haven't, you can't put it on.

Only twenty minutes or so have passed by the time I'm out the door and into the car. It's not a long trip to work – perhaps 150 yards or so to the edge of the car park overlooking the water; not that I can see the firth, for it is still dark. Open the tailgate of the car and sit down to pull on the waders. Time was we all wore thigh boots ('Bulldog' brand were the best, though too expensive except for skipper's wear), preferably black ones since greens are mostly for rod fishermen – but for some time now I have gone over to 'chesties'. They are warmer on those days, pretty much the norm now, when there isn't a lot of action, and more convenient when mooring the boat at the end of the tide and wading back through deep water. So, tuck the trousers into the stockings, haul the boots on, pick up bag and jackets and start walking down the shore.

Dawn is still an hour away, but the sun never dips far down in the Highlands so close to midsummer, and there is enough light, once my eyes are accustomed to it, to pick my way across the weed, mud, sand and stones of the ebb. There isn't a breath of wind, and the air feels soft. The oystercatchers and redshanks are piping away, and as I get close to the water's edge I can hear the very faint hissing of the tide ebbing and uncovering more of their feeding grounds. These shore birds live by the rhythm of the tides, not the sun. If the tide has ebbed, whether it is night or day, they will be out there feeding.

Now I can just make out the cairn and the boat beside it. It always looks, in this dim light, as if the two are one and that the boat is aground. But I am used to the illusion, and in fact the cairn is only just up, and the boat is floating free. At least it is not one of those foggy mornings when the haar is so thick that there is no distinction between air and water; ten yards out, the cairn disappears and you lose all sense of direction. Now I wade

Looking west just before dawn, the moon still in the sky.

out to the cairn, pull the boat in, pile my gear into the bow, fit one set of oars on their pins, untie the rope, row out thirty yards or so and drop anchor.

It will be some time before the crew appear; it is too dark to see fish yet. I have taken with me one of the cheap chairs which we use on the cairn. They are a sign of the times – that shots are now fewer and farther between, and that the crew are getting older and creakier. I set the chair up on the decking in the bow, make a roll-up and pour myself a cup of tea. These are some of my best times on the water, alone in the boat with just the firth and its inhabitants for company. The water is flat calm and the morning is dead quiet, apart from the birds and the occasional low hum as headlights sweep along the main road half a mile away across the bay. Now and again there is a splash. It's still too dark to see these, but most of them are the 'plop' of a troutie's vertical jump; only once is there the much more ragged sound of a grilsie's travelling leap behind me, and I whip round; this time I can see the mark of the jump, quite close, but there's not enough light to see him swimming.

Now there is a perceptible brightness in the east, and by crouching low, so that my eyes are almost at the level of the water, I can almost see the surface well enough to spot fish. But no fish appear. Instead, I have a very unusual visitor. About thirty feet away, directly off the mouth of the Skiach, a small something pops up in the water. I strain to see what it is – a duck? A baby seal? It moves closer, and I catch sight of a small whiskery head. It's an otter, the only one I have ever seen in the firth, although I know they live on all the rivers; Eddie and Chris once had a close encounter with one which disturbed them canoodling on the riverbank near the ford. This one and I eyeball each

Dawn at Kiltearn. (*Robert Blake*)

other for a few seconds, then I make an involuntary movement, and the otter dives in a flash. I never see it again.

It is now light enough to see fish, and I begin to wonder where the crew are. An eider and her brood of six ducklings approach the boat and swim past me just feet away. Perhaps they don't recognize boat or human, or just think the object in the water is another cairn. Now they are almost close enough to reach out and touch. A heron flaps in from the Black Isle, then glides down and alights on the Slippery Stones, where he perches on the edge and, like me, starts to watch the water.

The distinctive engine note of his big Honda motorcycle announces the arrival of Rik, and close behind him, down the brae from the main road, come the lights of Steve K's van. In ten minutes they are wading across to the cairn.

'Aye, aye, coff. Nice morning for it.'

'Yeah, good. I've heard fish already.'

The cairn is now well up, so much so that the water in front of it is getting very shallow.

'I think we'll head out.'

We all climb into the boat and row to the outside cairn. It's a tricky landing here: there's a deep pot at the back of the cairn, and an unwary disembarkation can land you in water up to your waist. But Steve negotiates it safely, and we leave him there with a

Steve K and Rik watch the water. Steve is standing on a thwart which brings him up to the same height as Rik. The bow oars, far too good for us, were made of oak by Robert Blake. (*JH*)

chair, his piece-bag and the end of the hint rope, while Rik and I row out twenty yards or so, throw out the anchor and start watching the water.

Pretty soon the sun comes up, an apricot ball over Invergordon. This could make the sight very tricky looking east, but there's a thin veil of cloud around, and we do not have to look directly at it. We have a shot of a couple of fish coming out of the Foulis bay – sneaky, as they often are in the calm; we only spot them when they are very close, so there's a last-minute scramble. And now it is even getting too shallow at the outside cairn, so we move to the Slippery Stones, dislodging the heron and finding the remains of his breakfast, some empty crab shells. By now, Rik and Steve have swapped places, and soon we have another shot, of three, coming from the east this time and motoring nicely along, parallel with the shore.

It really is a big tide today; now the cairns are all high and dry and the edge of the ebb is just a straight line stretching on towards Balconie. When it's like this, who can say where the boundary is between the Foulis and Balconie stations? It's meant to be the line of the Skiach, but the river is hundreds of yards away. So we decide to do a little trespassing. The tide is still going out, although more slowly, and while I take the hint rope and walk along the shore, Rik and Steve lift the anchor and float gently eastwards, watching for fish as we go.

The tactic works. We have two more small shots, and end up very nearly opposite the site of the Balconie bothy. Then the tide turns – as ever on these big springs, there is virtually no period of slack water – and with it the sun comes out and a little breeze strikes up from the east. This all conveniently helps us to float slowly back to the cairns, the bow of the boat heaped up with jackets and sweaters discarded as the day warmed. Very soon the tide gets a grip and is galloping in. Although the water looking west is perfect for fishing – a light, steady breeze with enough south in it to push the fresh water into the bay – we get little time on each of the cairns, just enough on the inside one to pick up a shot of three more.

Before long, it's time to go. We fit the fish – twelve grilsies – into two sacks, and I land crew and fish on the edge of the ebb. It's a Friday, the last tide of the fishing week, so we have to carry the oars up, too – otherwise the boat might be too much of a temptation to kids or other weekend wanderers. It's quite a load to take up the beach. We form a chain to carry the sacks and each of us puts an oar on his shoulder (big Rik takes two, of course). Halfway, we stop and change hands.

Back on dry land, we share out the fish – two each to the crew, the rest to the skipper and the boat – and make for Keith's conservatory, some strong coffee, butteries and raspberry jam, and a convivial smoke.

A good morning's work.

34

Decline and Fall

It's Tuesday, 21 July 2020, low water is at 7.30 am, it's a fine big tide (0.7m) and there's a gentle westerly breeze on the water. But I'm not there. For only the second July in forty-five years, I am not standing in the coble watching for fish. I'm sitting at my desk in London, writing this.

From the moment I started fishing, more than half a century ago now, there has been concern about declining numbers of fish and threats to their future. In 1962 the Hunter Report made a number of radical proposals aimed at reforming the regulation of salmon fisheries, both rod-and-line and netting, although very few of these became law. The committee recommended banning all drift-netting for salmon (using the loathsome gill net), and a ban was indeed introduced in Scottish waters, but the highly productive Northumberland drift-net fishery (gill nets again) continued to operate. In 1967 the Atlantic Salmon Trust was founded in response to two particular threats: the spread of UDN (ulcerative dermal necrosis), a disgusting skin disease (I have seen fish with their heads covered in lesions and fungus) which affects salmon in fresh water and can kill them before they spawn; and the opening of an uncontrolled drift-net fishery off Greenland which was taking hundreds of tons of fish.

In the 1970s another high-seas fishery for salmon started, in the form of long-lining off the Faroe Islands, and by 1981 it was taking 1,000 tons of fish every year, to add to the several thousand tons caught by the Greenland drift-netters. In 1989, Orri Vigfússon, an Icelandic entrepreneur and environmentalist, established the North Atlantic Salmon Fund (NASF) to 'restore the abundance of wild salmon that formerly existed on both sides of the North Atlantic'. He succeeded in raising enough money to buy out the Greenland quotas, and introduced a scheme whereby the Faroese were effectively paid not to fish.

This was the first of many restrictions and closures of commercial salmon fisheries. By 1988 the start of the weekly close time in Scotland had already moved from midday on Saturday to 6.00 pm on Friday, and the Atlantic Salmon Trust had begun to purchase netting rights and close stations down; they bought the Balconie rights in 1987 on behalf of the Conon District Fishery Board, and by this time all the stations I have worked, except for Kiltearn, had gone. In 2015 came a dramatic change, when all coastal netting (bag nets and stake nets) was banned in Scotland, initially for three years but now indefinitely. This was welcomed by rod fishermen (of course) and greeted with dismay by many coastal communities, such as the seaboard villages of Easter Ross, where the bag nets were almost the last form of local fishing left. Then in 2018 the drift-netters of Northumberland, three-quarters of whose catch was estimated to have been heading for Scottish rivers, fished their last ever season.

Apart from a handful of haaf-netters on the Solway, the few surviving net and coble stations were thus the only salmon net fisheries left standing. In the firth, that meant Kiltearn and the two banging stations above the bridge, but here, too, the writing was on the wall. In July 2018, Rod, Jonathan and I put the boat in the water, complete with new net, in preparation for, though without any great expectations of, another season – in recent years we had caught so few that there had been a lot of quips about us being not in the fishing but in the fish conservation business. The boat safely launched, with a dram, on Kiltearn beach, and the trailer discreetly parked in the whins, we repaired to Keith's for coffee and to wait for the tide to go back, at which point we could get out to the cairn and, maybe, if the water looked all right, fish the tide.

Then my phone rang. It was Finnian, the young laird of Foulis, and he had some news for us.

'I've got this letter here, and I think it may be important for you.'

The letter came from Marine Scotland, the body charged by the Scottish government with protecting Scotland's coastal waters, and it said (I paraphrase):

Your returns for season 2017 [a total catch of eight fish!] show that you were fishing last year in a place where 'catch and release of all salmon and grilse was mandatory' [nobody told us]. I am writing to point out that you have been naughty boys and that you mustn't do it again this year. Any salmon or grilse caught should be returned to the water from which it came and with the least possible injury, and failure to do so will result in your kneecaps being removed and your boat and net confiscated. Etc, etc.

In other words, we could catch fish but we would have to put them back – like the rod fishermen. This was something of a facer, to say the least. I chewed it over, and decided on two courses of action. First, I rang Finnian.

'Look, Finn, about this letter. You haven't told me about it until next week. OK?'

He agreed, and this at least meant we could get a last week's fishing in. As it happened, although we didn't catch many, we saw more fish in that week than for several years past, including a couple of really nice-looking heads. The new net worked beautifully, a much easier pull for us pensioners than the heavy old one, some of which is now protecting Rod's strawberries. And at the end of the week, without particular ceremony or any tears, the boat came out of the water and went up to the arches at Foulis Mains, where she still sits, with the almost brand new net hanging over her. I sometimes say, only half jokingly, that she will stay there until the time comes for her to carry me on my Viking funeral.

My second step was to contact Marine Scotland. I wanted an explanation of what was going on and to discover whether there was any chance of an appeal. I got a helpful fellow on the phone who assured me that the letter meant what it said and that the regulations would be 'enforced' – in other words, the bailiffs would be looking out for us. He also sent me a good deal of paperwork explaining Marine Scotland's decision. What it boiled down to was this: as a conservation measure, based on estimates of returning and spawning fish, all of Scotland's rivers and estuaries have been placed into one of three categories. Category 1: some fish can continue to be killed. Category 2: action necessary to reduce exploitation. Category 3: mandatory catch and release. Currently, about 60 per cent of districts, including the Cromarty Firth, fall into Category 3. The classifications are reviewed every year, so during the winter I sent Marine Scotland this letter:

Balconie Lady in retirement.

I write to object to the rating of the Cromarty Firth as Category 3 (mandatory catch and release of salmon) for season 2019.

I have fished in the Firth for more than 50 years on a number of different sweep-netting stations, and since 2000 have been the tenant of the fishing at Kiltearn Point, near Evanton. In support of my objection I should like to point to the following:

- Our method of fishing is traditional and, I believe, unique. Sweep-netting stations are (or were) common, but I know of nowhere else fished in the same way. We spot fish by eye, only shooting the net when fish are seen, and then track them as they swim into the net. This skill has been handed down through generations of fishermen in the Firth and will be lost for good if we are unable to continue fishing. I am also sending you some extracts from an article published in *Archipelago* magazine which describes in more detail this very special fishing method and its particular attractions.
- As a quick look at the catch returns for the last few years will confirm (2014–2017 inclusive, fewer than 40 fish in total), Kiltearn is not and never will be a commercial station. Compared to Balconie Point, or the mouth of the Alness River (commercial stations now closed), relatively few fish strike the shore there. We fish for sport and for the very occasional fish for the pot.
- My landlords, Hector and Finnian Munro, strongly support my objection and wish to see this traditional and culturally significant form of fishing continue at Kiltearn.

- We have always fished according to the letter of the law – indeed, because of the way we fish, there is no inducement to break the law (as other sweep-netters have been known to do) by operating the net as a stationary 'trap' or fixed engine. Moreover, our presence on the shore is a deterrent to anyone attempting to set an illegal net in the area.
- I would be quite happy to accept a limit of some kind, either in time (i.e. fishing restricted to a month) or in catch (say, 25 fish), and we would be open to inspection at any time. Kiltearn is, in any case, only fishable at low tide, and we have generally fished for little more than four weeks; in other words, the station is only fished for about twenty tides a year.
- I note that the River Conon (the destination of virtually all the fish which pass Kiltearn Point) is currently rated as Category 1. In the light of this, it seems surprising that mandatory catch and release should be in force at Kiltearn.
- I accept the need for conservation measures to protect salmon stocks, but I believe that other factors (fish farming, predation by seals and dolphins, climate change, to name but three) pose a far greater threat than one small, traditional 'hobby' fishing station.

This was met with a dead bat by the civil servants, and the firth remains a 'Category 3' area. I have no expectation of this decision being reversed.

The last fish we ever caught, and a beauty, too.

35

Reflections

Every summer, I take a walk from Kiltearn down to Balconie Point and on to the ford. Once in a while, I go down the Yankee Pier at Alness, too, and have a look at the cairns. I have never seen fish – not even a jumper – on these occasions; there are now fewer of them, of course, but I never spend long there, so it's also a reminder that to catch fish you have to put the hours in.

Visiting Balconie is particularly poignant. The surroundings are much as they ever were – the old bothy, the Corsican pines, the Ordnance Survey trig point which I officially 'adopted' a few years ago and occasionally remember to give a coat of whitewash to, the track leading on past the lagoon to the ford. But the heart of it is missing – the bothy has gone. Until a few years ago you could still find the hearthstone, but now that has disappeared too, and it's difficult to tell exactly where the bothy itself once stood. A few yards to the east of its site, an elder bush has grown up just above the high water

What's left of the fishing. This image appears on the interpretive board set up for tourists at Balconie Point. (L to R) self, Stevie Web, Rik, Eddie. (*RR*)

mark, near where the old coble lay. We would have cut it down, of course, because it is right in the line of sight from the west wind bench. The only relic of our presence is what is known in the tourist trade as a piece of 'interp' – a notice board erected by the trackside bench describing and illustrating our fishing.

Sitting on the beach, I reflect on what is left of the fishing days. I always knew, of course, that there would come a time when I had to 'retire', but Marine Scotland took this decision out of my hands. Boat and net are still there, just in case … but the last fish boxes now do duty as shelves in the garden shed; my polaroids, once crucial tools for water-watching as many of the photographs in the book will testify, have been relegated to the car; my Norwegian sweater has been consigned to a box under the bed, along with a collection of tatty flannel 'fishing' shirts which Jan will not allow to be seen in public; my Opinel knife, rusty from gutting and scaling many a fish at the edge of the firth, sits unused in a drawer; my netting needles, now loaded with garden twine, are in the allotment shed; my hip flask is gathering dust on the shelf above my desk – I have just taken it down and discovered it contains a last dram, maturing there since July 2018.

As winter turned to spring, I always used to experience a series of fishing dreams. In the nature of these things, they were usually at one remove from reality – rowing a shot in a canal, say, or set on a Balconie Point which housed a whole row of fisherman's shacks. The dead fishers walk again, too, and I have spent time with both Doug and Stevie Web. I still have these dreams from time to time, but while they once tended to be tinged with unease – I can't raise a crew, the boat is sinking, fish are swimming out of the net – nowadays they are more peaceful. The last time, we were fishing a monster tide in sunny weather on a fantasy sandbank three-quarters of the way to the Black Isle. The mood is something like the last days of August used to be – the season behind me, lying in bed late into the morning listening to a robin's mournful autumn song outside the window but knowing that, come May, I would be back on the water again.

Even if I am not there to see it, I would like to think that one day the fish will return in numbers and that netsmen may learn again how to spot them and catch them in the waters of the firth. Salmon are such important indicators of the health of both fresh water and the seas. They spend over half their life in fresh water, where they absolutely must have high levels of dissolved oxygen to survive. Many of Britain's southern and eastern rivers are not in good shape (a recent assessment concluded that the salmon populations of almost two thirds of the main salmon rivers in England and Wales are 'at risk'), but most northern and western ones can still offer our fish a clean home. And although man has polluted many salmon rivers, it is within our power to oversee their recovery.

However, salmon also depend on the sea, where they do nearly all of their feeding and growing, and it seems that man is currently doing his best to spoil this too. Global heating, over-fishing, the 200 million tons of microscopic plastic particles which the UK's National Oceanographic Centre estimates to be swilling about in the Atlantic; these things are already affecting our fish and will continue to do so until humanity properly wakes up to what it is doing to the planet.

Back in 2007, I wrote an article about the fishing for *Archipelago* magazine. Even then, it had changed beyond recognition, and the piece has a distinctly valedictory tone, as this adapted extract shows:

These were the days [the early 1980s] when all the stations were being worked: Buller and Doug at Alness, Hamish and Davy on the Crown cairn, Dave, big Rik and Steve at Kiltearn. Saturday midday in the pub, when the fishing week was over, could be quite an occasion. But already the writing was on the wall. Fish farming on a big scale had begun, and the poor flabby creatures turned out by the farms undercut the market for the real thing. Prices reached their peak in 1979 and never recovered. High seas fishing, much of it illegal, took increasing numbers of fish, and the

An evening tide on the cairn. (*RR*)

farms were spreading parasites and disease to the wild stock. Angling interests began to exert pressure to shut netting stations, and one by one they were bought out or closed down.

So the stations closed and the fishers went their different ways, into retirement, or to other more reliable occupations. But one station remained open, Kiltearn at the mouth of the Skiach, part of the long stretch of shore where the rights belong to Munro of Foulis. We don't want to catch a lot of fish here – not that we would turn away from a big shot if we saw it coming, you understand – and what we do get just about keeps the crew happy and leaves a few over for the smoker. The bothy has gone, burned by vandals, and Balconie Point has been opened up to dog walkers by a footbridge and a network of efficiently signed paths. The early mornings, once so quiet that you could hear the pigeons cooing across the water on the Black Isle, are now polluted by the hum of traffic on the new A9. But when we are out on the water, smoking, talking, watching, always hoping for the black peak which signals a big head swimming our way, nothing has really changed. Many of the old fishers still come down for a tide, and every year we see new faces as well. Last season was shocking – the rain didn't help, the rivers were high throughout July and fish did not hang around in the firth to be caught. But there's always next year. Of course, most of us are getting on in years, but as long as the fishing is there and we can stand, I suspect we will, come July, be pulling on our waders, shouldering our piece-bags and walking down the beach to the boat to go fishing.

In memory of Buller who taught us all, old Paul who saw fish coming over, Doug and Stan who went before their time, and Davy who died with his boots on.

'There's always next year' … that no longer holds true. A part of my life – my other life, whatever it was that I was doing in the off-season – has gone. But the memories remain.

36

The Last Fishers

Rik Parke

The very last word goes to Rik, his elegiac poem.

Oars sigh restlessly,
Bowing in lopsided rhythm,
Blades keen to knife the tension,
The skin between lost and seen.

A few men stand stranded
On a whale-backed cairn,
Eyes devout to the smallest flicker,
The jabble of fin under wave.

The wishful, the prayered
Hope of one last great fish,
Green-backed and urgent,
Shedding scales through mesh.

Whispered hints of the loss
Beneath the rippled mirror,
The fat hag fish bloated
On sunk dolphin,

The sharp skulls of razorbill
Spat onto the shingle shore,
Beaks gape wide, begging
For more than stones.

And the men still stand,
Fuzzy in the last light,
Boat riding high under
Dry net and hare moon.

Glossary

Backboard	The flat stern of a coble on which the net rests
Bag	Looser and stronger section in the middle of a sweep net
Birl	To revolve. The swirl in the water made by a rapidly turning fish
Black jock	Cormorant
Blank	A shot which fails to catch fish
Boat rope	Rope attaching the net to the boat
Bothy	Accommodation for fishermen during the season
Cairn	A mound of stones, gravel and sand constructed to work a net from at low tide
Channel	The deep middle of the firth, beyond the reach of even the biggest ebb tides
Coble	Flat-bottomed, wide-bodied rowing boat
Craic	Conversation, socializing ('Having the craic') or news/gossip ('What's the craic?')
Cruives	Fixed fish traps in a river
Cudplucker	Monkfish
Donkey	A big salmon (over about 10lbs) which has spent more than one winter at sea
Factor	Manager of a Highland estate
Finnock	A small sea trout
Fixed engine	A stationary net or trap for fish, e.g. bag nets, stake nets
Float rope	The buoyed upper rope of a sweep net
Gadgie	A man, bloke, chap
Ghillie	Someone who acts as an attendant and adviser to a rod fisherman
Gills	The respiratory organs of fish, protected by flaps of tissue, the gill covers. If a fish gets its head through a net, these can get stuck when it attempts to withdraw. It is then said to be 'gilled', and 'gill nets' are designed to catch fish in this way
Girnel	A storehouse for agricultural produce
Gloss	Area of calm, shiny fresh water among ripples
Grilse/grilsie	Smaller salmon, which has spent just one winter at sea
Ground rope	The weighted bottom rope of a sweep net

Gunwale	Upper edge of a boat's side
Haar	Sea fog
Head	A shoal of fish, also the mark on the surface made by a shoal or the direction a shoal is swimming in ('Are you getting his head?')
Heave	The mark of a good head of fish
Henry	A seal
Hint rope	The rope between the boat and the shore
Horn	Projection from the gunwale either side of the bow, used to attach the anchor rope and to hold when towing and manoeuvring the coble
Jabble	Disturbed water surface caused by fluky winds or wind against tide in which seeing fish is difficult
Jumper	A fish which jumps clear of the water
Kelt	A fish which has spawned and is attempting to return to the sea
Lacers	Seaweed resembling long coarse hairs
Laird	Owner of a Highland estate
Loon	A boy or apprentice
Lumpy calm	Calm water but with a swell to it, in which it is difficult to see fish
Neap	Small (tide)
Net and coble	Our fishing technique; sweep-netting or beach seine
Parr	Juvenile salmon in fresh water
Piece	Sandwiches or packed lunch, kept in a 'piece-bag'
Redd	The 'nest' of gravel in which salmon lay their eggs
Scalder	Lion's mane jellyfish
Shake	Mark on the surface which might be made by fish
Shot/shottie	Several meanings: the act of fishing ('Rowing the shot'); the catch ('A big shot of fish'); the area where you fish ('The shot has a good sandy bottom')
Skoker	A single fish ('skulker')
Slippery Stones	An old cairn consisting of big stones covered in seaweed
Smolt	Juvenile salmon which has become silvery and descended the river to go to sea
Snag	Anything on which the net catches. Also a sausage
Spring	Big (tide)
Springer	Large salmon which enters the river early in the year
Tack	When the net catches on itself and fails to come off smoothly or hang correctly in the water ('There's a tack in the net')
Tangle	Kelp
Tattie graip	A potato-digging fork
Thwart	Seat in a boat

Trout, troot, trootie   Sea trout
Ware   Seaweed
Water   Mark made by a head of fish ('He's making a good water', 'I'm not getting his water')
Whins   Gorse, broom
Wing   One side of the net. The bag is set between the two wings

Acknowledgements

My first thanks, for their companionship on the water over many years, go to these surviving regulars: Robert Blake, Dick Clarke, Jodie Eaglesham, Jonathan Harding, Steve Kerr, Dave McLachlan, Paul Major, Rik Parke, Rod Richard, Eddie Scott, Bobby Smart, Steve Sutcliffe. Apologies to anyone who feels left out – so many people have fished with us over the years, but the line had to be drawn somewhere.

Thank you to the following, for the use of their poems, paintings or photographs: Ian and Mary Black, Robert Blake, Fionna Chalmers, Gina Chamier, Tif Eccles, the family of George Huntley, John Lawrence-Jones, Andrew McNeillie, Rik Parke, Eddie Scott. Special mentions go to Jonathan Harding, Dave McLachlan and Rod Richard, who between them supplied many of the photographs in the book, and to John Lawrence-Jones, whose professional help in preparing the images was hugely valuable. John's superb portrait of a couple of fish appears on the front cover of the book. Photograph credits, unless spelled out, are shown as follows: FC – Fionna Chalmers, JH – Jonathan Harding, DM – Dave McLachlan, RR – Rod Richard, ES – Eddie Scott. If uncredited, images are either mine or in the public domain. I apologize to anyone whose photographs I have misidentified or failed to credit.

For their hospitality over many fishing seasons I am very grateful to my sister, Antoinette Gordon, to Keith Kennedy, provider of Scotland's most luxuriously appointed fishing bothy, and to that queen of guest house landladies, Romay Garcia. Keith also kindly allowed us to leave oars and other gear at his house, and to park the boat there for many winters.

Hector Munro of Foulis has been a most generous and helpful landlord over many seasons at Kiltearn, as well as an occasional fisherman himself. He has rescued us from disaster on a number of occasions, as has Finnian Munro, another fisherman at one time.

Kit Kennedy kept the *Balconie Lady* in a fine state of repair for many seasons, and Steve Kerr and Brian Knox revived her with great skill in her hour of need.

To my wife Jan I owe thanks for many things, especially her love and support for nearly half a century. A professional editor, she solved many IT problems for me, acted as a sounding-board for my ideas, read the book in manuscript and kept me from committing errors of both style and judgement. Above all, over many years, she suffered my absence on the firth for weeks on end without complaint.

The following people also read the book in manuscript and made helpful suggestions and encouraging comments: David Burnett, Pete Duncan, Andrew McNeillie, Carol O'Brien, Rik Parke, Eddie Scott.

I am grateful to Alistair Stenhouse for allowing me to read and to quote from his most interesting and comprehensive MSc dissertation, *The Archaeology of Coastal Salmon Fishing in Easter Ross: an industry in terminal decline*, and I look forward to hearing the results of his further research in the area.

I owe a huge debt of gratitude to all at Pen & Sword, colleagues for many years and now in a new guise as my publishers, especially the following: Henry Wilson for taking the book on in the first place; Matt Jones for his sense of humour and calm efficiency at the centre of things; Jon Wilkinson for a beautiful jacket design; and Mat Blurton for his excellent design work.

Messrs Google and Wikipedia have been my helpful friends, as ever, but I have also consulted the following books:

David Alston, *Ross and Cromarty: a Historical Guide* (Birlinn, 1997)
Marinell Ash, *This Noble Harbour* (John Donald, 1991)
Albert C. Baugh & Thomas Cable, *A History of the English Language* (Routledge & Kegan Paul, 1984)
John Bennett, *The Summer Crew* (Spey publishing, 2020)
Fred Buller, *The Domesday Book of Giant Salmon* Vols I & II (Constable, 2007, 2010)
Jessie Macdonald & Anne Gordon, *Down to the Sea* (Ross & Cromarty Heritage Society, 1990)
Norman Matheson, *A Speyside Odyssey* (Matador, 2019)
Derek Mills, *Scotland's King of Fish* (1980)
Iain A. Robertson, *The Salmon Fishers* (The Medlar Press, 2013)
Charles St John, *Wild Sports and Natural History of the Highlands* (1848)
Richard Shelton, *To Sea & Back* (Atlantic Books, 2009)
Jim Walker, *By Net and Coble* (Blackhall Press, 2006)
W. J. Watson, *Place-Names of Ross and Cromarty* (1904)
Henry Williamson, *Salar the Salmon* (Penguin, 1949)